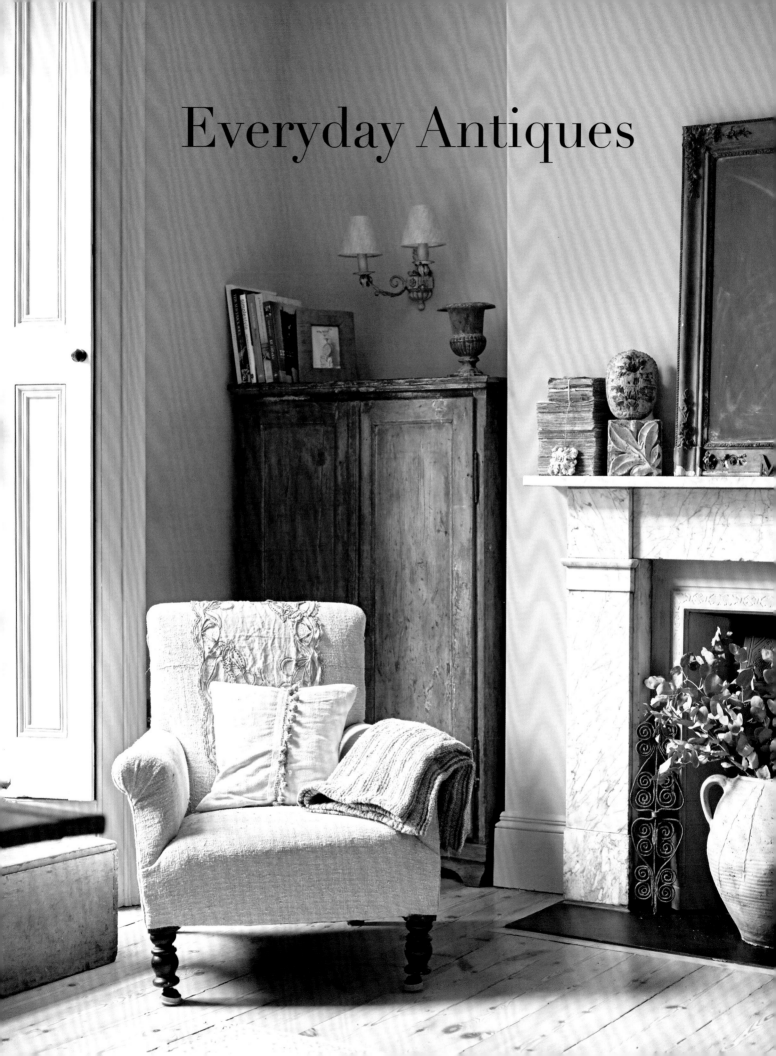

Everyday Antiques

Everyday Antiques

INVITING HOMES WHERE OLD MEETS NEW

Katherine Sorrell

RYLAND PETERS & SMALL

LONDON • NEW YORK

Senior designer Toni Kay
Editor Sophie Devlin
Picture research Jess Walton
Production manager Gordana Simakovic
Senior commissioning editor Annabel Morgan
Creative director Leslie Harrington

For photography credits, see page 188.

Published in 2024 by Ryland Peters & Small
20–21 Jockey's Fields
London WC1R 4BW
and
341 East 116th Street
New York, NY 10029

www.rylandpeters.com

10 9 8 7 6 5 4 3 2 1

ISBN 978-1-78879-614-9

A CIP record for this book is available
from the British Library.

Library of Congress CIP data has been applied for.

Printed and bound in China

FSC
MIX
Paper | Supporting
responsible forestry
FSC® C008047

Contents

Introduction

In today's mass-produced, homogenized world, we're all seeking ways to create a home that feels authentic, nurturing and uniquely our own. And antiques and vintage items can help us do just that. Each piece of old furniture, textile or decorative accessory, whether carefully sourced from a specialist dealer, purchased via an online auction, picked up for free on a recycling website or sourced in a market or charity shop, brings with it a quality that simply can't be replicated by a trip to a chain store. From the clean lines of a mid-century modern chair to the cheerful colours of a 1930s tea set, from a sturdy Victorian chest of drawers to a salvaged factory lamp, every antique or vintage piece possesses its own fascinating history, patina of age and richness of character.

Another advantage of antiques and secondhand pieces, and one that's highly pertinent today, is their sustainability. They're the epitome of recycling and 'green' thinking, of buying for quality and durability. Most of them are far better made than their modern equivalents, using quality materials and high levels of craftsmanship that will ensure they last for years to come.

Living with antiques needn't be expensive. While some may want to save up to invest in a single, gorgeous piece, it's easy to find inexpensive antiques and vintage items for your space. This is not a book about investing, but about buying things you love and which will enhance your life, make your home feel special and, in most cases, are useful, too. If there is one thing this book does, it is – hopefully – to demonstrate that antiques of all kinds, at all price points, singly or en masse, can be used in ways that are attractive and appealing, and not fussy or pretentious. Style-wise, too, antiques vary so much and, as shown on the following pages, can be employed in schemes that have a rustic or an industrial vibe, a retro feel, a dash of drama or a simple and understated effect. They are impressively versatile.

Here we focus on the main spaces of the living room, kitchen, dining room, bedroom and bathroom, and look in detail at antique and vintage furniture, lighting, textiles and decorative accessories. The possibilities are endless and I hope you'll be inspired to create a unique home in which the past meets the present to truly reflect your personality.

THE
SPACES

OPPOSITE Demonstrating the quality of its original construction, a partially reupholstered French tub chair sits very naturally in this light-filled room with tall sash windows. Teamed with a pretty tripod wine table and an adjustable vintage clamp lamp, it's an inviting spot for reading in the sunshine.

LIVING

Adding a smattering of antique and vintage pieces to a living room will create an effect that's both elegant and eclectic. Such pieces don't have to be rare, grand or expensive, but older items that have developed a patina of age will bring interest and detail to any interior. Give antiques space to breathe and offset them with modern pieces, plants, books and textiles for living rooms with soul and balance.

Keep it simple

There is luxury in simplicity, and a tranquil living space offers a welcoming retreat at the end of a busy day. If a restful interior is your thing, antiques will bring quiet charm to such a room.

Introducting antique, vintage or retro furnishings into your living room will add a sense of warmth and charm, as well as the appealing characteristics of the aged, the worn and the well-loved. Even in the most modern and boxy of rooms, one or two old pieces will tone down hard lines, banish any sense of sterility and provide a mood of easy-going comfort.

The starting point for a relaxed and simple scheme is a sense of space – this aesthetic can't be achieved in cluttered or overfilled rooms. Airy, light interiors are obviously the ideal, but even if your living room is small and dark there are ways in which to increase its potential. Paint the walls a pale, muted shade, choosing a tone that is not too cool or clinical, and use light-coloured flooring – wood, carpet or natural matting (you could consider liming or painting dark or stained floorboards). Minimize the window treatments, opting for plain curtains in heavy linen or wool, or simple blinds/shades. If you have beautiful views or are not overlooked, you might even want to get rid of window coverings altogether. Optimise storage – built in or free-standing – so that inessentials can be kept out of sight and your eyes fall instead on useful or decorative objects that you love to have around.

With the bones of your living room in place, consider the furnishings. The essential is a capacious sofa or, if space allows, a pair of them. In small rooms, however, you might prefer a couple of armchairs that are large enough to curl up in, a 1.5-seater love-seat or even a chaise longue, which will add a note of languid elegance to even the most pared-down scheme. If you're opting for second-hand seating, make sure there are no broken springs or torn upholstery. Old sofas and chairs, especially in leather, can have a delightfully inviting silhouette, but sometimes re-covering, in a hard-wearing plain cotton ticking, cotton velvet or woven wool, results in a great improvement. Again, pale colours (although impractical in homes where there are children or pets) will emphasize a calm and tranquil aesthetic.

As for storage, an antique cupboard or cabinet is always a useful addition to the mix. A Victorian pine blanket chest or a steamer trunk holds plenty and makes a superb contrast with modern furnishings, as does a low, mid-century modern sideboard/credenza. For an impressive focal point and a change of tone, look for a decorative piece, such as an antique French armoire with carved detailing, or an old English chest, perhaps painted or adorned with pretty handles.

When buying old or antique furniture, look out for well-made pieces in good-quality materials and simple, understated colours. Natural materials have their own innate integrity, and are almost always superior to synthetic ones. In a simple living room, the seductive textures of grained wood, patinated leather and crisp cotton or linen will combine to create a reassuringly timeless atmosphere. Combining these materials with neutral shades of white, cream, stone and grey makes for relaxing surroundings, although you may wish to include an occasional dash of contrasting colour to delight the eye – perhaps some old chintz sourced on eBay and made into cushion covers, a vintage Welsh blanket used as a sofa throw, some smoky 1970s glassware

Calming shades of white, cream, ivory and taupe mingle with the textures of timber, wool and twinkling cut glass, creating a relaxed room that is very easy to spend time in. The glazed alcove cupboards offer a great opportunity to showcase favourite vintage finds.

With a huge double-height window, pale walls and a light timber floor, this room is inherently bright and airy. The solid dark colour of the modular sofas is grounding, while their sleek lines complement the minimal look. An adjustable machinist's wall lamp and industrial-style coffee table provide appealing contrast, as do the organic lines of a potted fig.

The swooping wooden arms of an Art Deco lounge chair complement the boxy shapes of a low modern sofa and a sideboard on slender legs. Chairs such as these were mass-produced during the 1930s and 40s and are easily sourced on eBay and other vintage furniture websites.

OPPOSITE The all-white walls and pale floor of this Paris apartment emphasize a feeling of space. A pair of classic Le Corbusier Petit Confort armchairs mingle with interesting flea-market finds that draw the eye.

or a monochrome 1960s print. For a truly simple look it's best to limit the number of accessories, but displaying a few favourite pieces that express your personality, whether they be centuries old or more recent treasures, has an appealing effect.

Last but not least, consider the way in which lighting can alter a living space. Discreet low-voltage downlighters, either set into the ceiling or surface mounted, make excellent task lights, casting enough light for reading or writing and to showcase prized ornaments and artworks. These can be supplemented with attractive period fittings that possess more character, such as a classic Anglepoise lamp or a floor lamp with an Edwardian-style fringed silk or milk glass shade. Don't forget that the soft, flickering glow cast by multiple candles is the most restful and flattering light of all.

When putting together a simple and relaxed yet modern look, it's essential to balance the elements that will soften and relax with those that are more formal and structured. With the addition of the right antique or vintage pieces, your living room will marry up the grace of the past with the sophistication of the present.

ABOVE Furniture that is raised on slim legs allows more floor area to be seen and instantly creates a sense of space, while glass and metal bounce light around a room. Here, vintage gilt-framed mirrors complement a modern sofa and coffee table and a Bertoia Diamond chair designed in 1952.

LEFT Limed wooden floorboards and a plain, almost austere backdrop give this London loft a contemporary feel, in spite of traditional seating in worn leather and chintz. This look is inexpensive and easy to recreate, relying on lack of clutter and the impact of spots of colour in a light-filled room for effect.

In this Long Island farmhouse, a fresh white slipcover has given a second-hand sofa a new lease of life, blending perfectly with white-painted walls and ceiling beams, sheer blinds and wide, original floorboards. The coffee table came from a yard sale, and the antique pine cabinet conceals the TV.

OPPOSITE Burnished-plaster walls give texture, warmth and depth to this living room, in which a mid-century modern daybed is teamed with elaborate glass and wrought-iron coffee tables, interesting lighting and a pair of eye-catching portraits. Touches of gilt and metal emphasize the sense of luxury. .

RIGHT What could be more glamorous than a combination of plaster-pink and gold? Here, a gold silk sofa and a gilt-framed portrait complement the soft shade of the Georgian wall panelling.

Make a statement

If you are drawn to dramatic, even theatrical interiors, unusual antique and vintage pieces can take centre stage in any home, be it a new build apartment or a centuries-old cottage. Tone them down for glamour and elegance; dial them up for high-voltage opulence.

Thanks to their unique lines and unusual finishes, some pieces of vintage furniture are guaranteed to turn heads. For a straightforward way to make a statement or to provide a bold finishing touch, look for a single oversized, ornate piece that will draw the eye. A huge gilt-framed mirror, for example, can be propped on a mantelpiece or against a wall, or a stunning vintage Murano chandelier can bring the wow factor. Allow pieces like this to be the centre of attention by keeping the surroundings simple – think sanded floorboards and Roman blinds/shades.

If you're a self-confessed maximalist, on the other hand, you may want to mix and match several pieces that share similar attributes – a curving gilt-legged 1950s table, for example,

will sit happily alongside another item that has the same qualities, such as shapely glassware or an antique chaise longue.

Make a statement by contrasting antiques with strong background colour and lavish textiles. All-over colour is full of impact, while splashes of deep, rich shades – berry reds, midnight blues or chocolate browns – will instantly create an atmosphere of indulgence. Luxurious fabrics such as velvet, silk, faux fur and metallic organza are a great addition to the mix. Think about layering colours, shapes, textures and patterns, with finishing touches including such decorative elements as beading, fringing, patterned rugs and large paintings. With ingenuity rather than spending a fortune, the result will be a living room that is a feast for the eyes.

ABOVE AND ABOVE RIGHT Bring on the drama with a very dark painted room, whether charcoal, navy or even black. These deep, rich colours look fabulous when teamed with natural wooden floorboards and, provided there is enough natural light, the room need not appear gloomy. Vintage pieces can work incredibly well in a scheme of this type, whether it's an Eames-style chair from the 1950s or a Hollywood Regency wheatsheaf coffee table from the 1960s. For interest and coordination, complement straight, blocky shapes with curves and scrolls, use minimal pattern and add judicious touches of burnished metal to lighten the scheme.

OPPOSITE The combination of deep grey, blue and crimson with an unexpected pop of orange is mouthwatering and very liveable. The balanced table lamp in typical 1950s style is, though a relatively small element of the scheme, very much a focal point.

OPPOSITE An oversized paper lampshade is the focal point of this eclectic living room, while the ornate 19th-century French mirror casually propped on the mantelpiece adds to the panache of the scheme. The mix of furnishings includes a mirror-ball floor lamp, a pair of vintage Ligne Roset Togo velvet sofas and a 1960s leather and tubular metal sling chair.

RIGHT The ornate carving of a pair of Louis XV-style armchairs brings a tactile detail to this otherwise sleek and neutral contemporary living space, while the gold mirror, in stepped Art Deco style, adds a touch of glitz.

LEFT Sometimes all you need is a single, beautiful piece to create a strong style statement. Here, an antique French chair with a squashy oversized cushion is the picture of comfort by the fire in this panelled room. The convex mirror and the twin-armed gilt wall light are delightful details, adding visual interest to the simple space.

ABOVE Art and accessories can be the making of even the smallest rooms, and there is much joy to be found in both sourcing them and arranging them. Vintage paintings, ceramics, glassware, ornaments and even beautifully bound books can all be picked up in charity shops, auctions and antiques markets, often at very little expense.

RIGHT The plain, flat front and tapering, splayed legs of this sideboard are quintessentially 1950s. The objects on display are mid-century, too, but the overall feel is fresh and modern, thanks to the contemporary prints on the wall above and the glossy vinyl flooring.

OPPOSITE The bold colours and fun shapes of mid-century modern furnishings bring warmth and interest to the grand, high-ceilinged living space in this new build house. A set of nesting tables, designed by Charlotte Perriand in 1951, is perhaps the most eye-catching addition, along with the sculptural Serge Mouille wall lamp, designed in 1953. Such pieces sit well alongside more traditional antiques, too.

Retro living

Furniture and accessories produced in the mid-twentieth century have a distinctive energy and optimism all of their own. Such pieces, whether modern classics or unassuming pieces by an anonymous designer, introduce appealing colours, interesting shapes and easy-going character.

R etro style can encompass designs from the 1930s through to the 1970s, but, for a striking look that is easy to put together, seek out pieces from the 1950s and early 1960s. Sofas, chairs and sideboards/credenzas from this period are slimline and clean-cut, raised off the floor on spindly, splayed legs. Colours are clear, and accessories such as clocks, vases and lamps tend towards the quirky and eye-catching.

A retro-inspired living room needs only one or two central pieces, though many people find that once they have bought one item they become fascinated with the period and simply can't stop. A long, lean sofa is a good start: anything from an expensive version by a well-known designer such as Florence Knoll to a re-edition by a major manufacturer or a lucky junk-shop or online marketplace find that needs re-upholstering. Keep the surroundings simple – think bare boards, parquet or rush matting on the floors, while white-painted walls will allow the distinctive silhouettes of these pieces to stand out. Sideboards/credenzas, coffee tables and armchairs from the period are key pieces, too, as are spindly lamps with conical shades and leggy side tables. If your living room is large enough to incorporate a dining table, you could offset it with a set of typically 1950s Scandinavian chairs.

Retro pieces integrate well with modern furnishings, thanks to their pared-down, delicate designs. They also make a strong statement in a period home, standing out against cornicing, ceiling roses and panelling as an unexpected contrast. And quirky accessories, used with care, add splashes of colour and fun. After all, this is a look that doesn't take itself too seriously, but creates a mix of old and new that is fresh, individual and enjoyable to live with.

ABOVE Teak sideboards, either British or Scandinavian, are an easily sourced classic of mid-century design, and work brilliantly in modern homes, offering the advantages of both practicality and good looks. With storage and a place for displays, this example looks gorgeous against a navy wall.

OPPOSITE The worn leather upholstery of this mid-century sofa is the epitome of comfort and style. The monochrome, swirling patterns of the table lamp are a great complement, offset by the drama of the bold artwork on the wall.

PAGE 30 The Scandi-retro style of this long, low sofa on legs complements the timber wall cladding. A mirrored coffee table and a natural hide rug make a striking textural contrast.

PAGE 31 The slightly battered crimson paint of this duo of vintage wood-and-leather cinema seats makes a luscious complement to the slightly more blueish red of the wall behind. The beautifully drawn horse chestnut lithograph by Jung Koch Quentell is an educational wall chart, printed in Germany between 1955 and 1965.

OPPOSITE This mid-century sideboard is adorned with a beautifully curated selection of ornaments and books, while a ceramic table lamp draws the eye. The bright blue dining chair adds another lovely jolt of colour.

ABOVE A pair of mid-century Florence Knoll-style armchairs are the focal point in this airy, open-plan living space, which also includes a selection of intriguing junk-shop finds.

ABOVE RIGHT In the same room, an array of ceramics and glassware from the mid-twentieth century, with whimsical outlines and vivid patterns, offers a dash of drama.

RIGHT A pair of elegant velvet-covered French Art Deco armchairs have a sumptuous feel that complements the curvy lines of the coffee table.

OPPOSITE A large coffee table made from an antique door takes centre stage in this serene living room with its wooden boarded ceiling. Limited colours emphasise delightful textures, including that of a vintage rice basket at the end of the sofa.

RIGHT In a Welsh farmhouse, a sheep made from reclaimed timber floorboards and inspired by an agricultural merchant's signpost has the appearance of antique folk art.

A rustic mood

Eclectic rustic style is one of the easiest ways to bring interest and warmth to an interior. Boxy rooms with little architectural detailing can be transformed with reclaimed wooden floors or simple tongue-and-groove clad walls and even ceilings, while cold, north-facing rooms can be cosied up with antique brown furniture, battered second-hand leather armchairs and natural fibre rugs. Add vintage folk art, baskets, lanterns and painted wooden surfaces to complete the look.

Texture is everything in a rustic scheme. Natural materials are at the heart of the look: wood, stone, clay and fibres such as linen, jute and rattan. Don't be deterred by rugged and distressed finishes; these will add structure and character and offset practical modern surfaces elsewhere. Keep floorboards unpolished, leave original tiles or stone floors uncovered or lay down rush matting to hide shiny laminate and introduce a sense of soul.

When it comes to colour, go for rich, earthy shades such as terracotta or indigo to transform a living space into a cosy cocoon. For a lighter look, opt for a single element of strong colour teamed with soft white or stone on the walls.

As for furniture, look for solid shapes and simple outlines – nothing too dainty. Club chairs and upholstered armchairs are perfect, while sturdy Victorian pine pieces such as linen presses or armoires are great for holding media and TV equipment, files or toys. Some have charming original paintwork, while others can be left au naturel or upcycled with a lick of paint. Modern sofas work well with old wooden tables (saw the legs off to make them the right height for a coffee table) or stools used as side tables. Add softness in the shape of undyed sheepskins or blankets hung over the back of sofas or chairs. And if you don't have a wood burner or open fire, mimic the effect by lighting candles everywhere.

BELOW An old wood burner warms the living room of this 17th-century Welsh cottage, with a wooden chest repurposed as a corner seat-cum-storage. The large rattan lamp contributes to the diversity of natural textures, which makes the room feel simple and cosy.

RIGHT This simple cabin retreat is filled with natural materials, including reclaimed floorboards and tongue-and-groove cladding. The collection of vintage furniture was found online and in flea markets and junk shops.

BELOW RIGHT Simple repairs to good-quality vintage furnishings can make them last and last, saving money and avoiding unnecessary landfill. The upholstery of this deeply buttoned sofa back has been mended several times, with assorted patches of modest fabric only adding to its rustic charm.

In a modern rural home built using traditional methods, exposed beams and antlers contribute to a sense of rustic grandeur. A palette of natural textures and tones of black, white, warm brown and a touch of red provides a wonderful sense of cohesion, and there's no doubting the comfort of the armchairs, with their beautifully worn leather, which were found in a French antiques shop.

LIVING *Style guide*

- Keep it simple – don't try to cram too much antique furniture into a living room, especially when mixing pieces from different periods. Start with a single statement piece, such as a classic Chesterfield or angular mid-century sofa.

- If you include one very strong pattern, keep the rest of the furnishings plain, avoiding clashes and allowing the pattern to stand out.

- To showcase furniture with interesting lines, keep wall treatments understated and in a pale colour.

- Old chairs from any era look marvellous re-upholstered in plain linen or cotton ticking fabric, which can bring a sense of cohesion to mismatched furniture. Alternatively, have slipcovers made for a more informal look.

- Lengths of old fabric, which are easily found on eBay or Etsy, can be made into window treatments or cushion covers. Against a plain backdrop, florals, toiles and 1960s prints look great, adding character and colour.

- For old furniture to work with newer designs, look for pieces that have a clean-lined feel. Bring together shapes that echo each other, such as the gentle curves of a tub chair and a 19th-century half-moon table.

- Scale is important. One oversized piece will make an impact, but avoid mixing lots of large and small pieces in one room – it will look crowded and cluttered. This goes for the details, too: if a table is chunky and solid with heavy, square legs, it will look wrong next to a chair of dainty proportions with slender, tapering legs.

- To avoid visual confusion, keep accessories to a minimum, choosing just one bold, dramatic item or a few quiet, timeless pieces arranged together rather than dotted around covering every surface.

- Use colour to coordinate. If a piece of wooden furniture is not working cohesively with the other elements of your living room, try painting it the same colour as the walls to help it blend in. Chalk paint requires little prep.

- Look for good-quality furniture with timeless style. Excellence in design, a high standard of craftsmanship and solid, natural materials provide common factors that unify different pieces, whatever their age.

regarde!

OPPOSITE A pair of mismatched crystal chandeliers, assorted metal signs, repurposed shelving and an industrial trolley combine happily in this eclectic kitchen, in which a tall, exposed-brick wall provides lovely texture and interest.

COOKING & EATING

The kitchen and dining room provide ample opportunities for living with antiques. Modern appliances look good contrasted with traditional utensils, while new dining tables can be teamed with vintage chairs, and fitted cabinetry offset by quirky period pieces. The addition of older furnishings results in rooms that are characterful but relaxed, the warm and friendly heart of a home.

OPPOSITE An old carpenter's workbench has been put into use as a kitchen island in this Brooklyn loft. Stainless-steel open shelving sourced from a commercial kitchen stockist provides plenty of storage space for pots, pans, glasses and more.

Urban industrial

Whether you live in a converted loft, a new-build townhouse or a 19th-century terrace, adding industrial-style antiques and vintage furnishings adds character, versatility and rugged good looks, while being unfussy and eminently practical.

Functional and utilitarian, this look draws inspiration from industrial spaces such as factories, laboratories, workshops or commercial kitchens. Old school furniture feels at home here, too. It's also forgiving if you're on a tight budget. Forget boxing in pipes and beams – exposed features such as columns, joists and brickwork provide an excellent backdrop to salvaged lights, furniture, accessories or kitchen equipment. Poured concrete floors or sanded floorboards are right for this look, while on the walls consider bare plaster, brick or subway tiles – perhaps making a feature of surface-mounted electrical conduits and copper pipework. In general, when it comes to surfaces, reclaimed or salvaged items, such as former science laboratory worktops or scaffolding-board shelves, are a great option, as are unpretentious materials such as scrubbed pine and stainless steel.

Against this no-nonsense backdrop, set furnishings with rugged, hard-working appeal. Keep elegant or decorative antiques for other rooms and instead look for sturdy benches, trolleys, cupboards or trestle tables that have worked hard in a previous life. For seating, factory machinist chairs are a good option, as are stackable ply school chairs – practical, cheap and good looking.

Contrasting textures are important. Balance distressed surfaces and well-worn pieces with softer, sleeker finishes to soften the ambience of an industrial style space. Continue the theme with lighting: old factory lamps, an adjustable desk lamp or a bulkhead wall lamp, for example. The finishing touch will be a selection of carefully chosen accessories, such as well-used wooden stools, piles of large chopping boards and French enamel signs on the wall.

OPPOSITE A pair of old factory pendant lights illuminates this bright dining area. The chairs are vintage chapel seats, solid, rich in colour and with a shelf for hymn books on the back.

RIGHT Pared down to the bare essentials, this calm kitchen features scrubbed floorboards, unfitted furniture and an old-fashioned fridge. The pale colour scheme adds to the serene effect, while the workbench used as a side table and the galvanized bin are both sturdy and practical.

BELOW In this white-walled loft space, metal-framed windows and a storage trolley on castors make a strong industrial-style statement, accentuated by the monochrome colour scheme. The iconic black chairs were designed by Norman Cherner in 1958.

ABOVE LEFT Vintage taps with exposed pipework add an instant industrial effect, especially when teamed with a sturdy salvaged tabletop basin.

ABOVE RIGHT A collection of vintage Indian lassi cups makes an unusual display as well as providing handy storage for a variety of smaller kitchen utensils.

BELOW LEFT The sleek nature of an inset, stainless-steel sink and streamlined modern tap is tempered by the charming row of vintage French enamel storage jars lined up on the shelf above.

BELOW RIGHT A vintage metal cabinet makes excellent storage in an unfitted kitchen. Here, the look is softened by the addition of prettily coloured wall tiles.

OPPOSITE Using vintage, reclaimed and upcycled furnishings means embracing their worn patina rather than attempting to disguise it. This 19th-century Cornish cottage kitchen has been furnished with antique and vintage finds that retain their beautifully weathered textures – and provide plenty of storage – while still being perfectly functional.

It is easy to add industrial-style storage to a kitchen or dining room in the form of shelving, baskets or a simple metal catering trolley. The latter can be piled with crockery, glassware, serving dishes or general cookware and wheeled around to anywhere you wish.

OPPOSITE A patterned-concrete floor and exposed beams give this converted Victorian tram depot in East London an eclectic, industrial vibe. The mix of vintage and modern furnishings, plus an array of house plants, softens the look.

OPPOSITE Fresh yellow paint enhances a floor-to-ceiling cupboard in this farmhouse kitchen. A comfortable Windsor chair sits next to the range cooker, with a Staffordshire dog on the shelf above as a finishing touch.

RIGHT A rich combination of natural textures is all-important in a country kitchen. Here, the gorgeous grain of a timber cabinet complements a wicker basket, rush-seated chairs and an assortment of patterned ceramics.

Simple country

Putting a new spin on country decor by adding antique and vintage pieces creates an interior that possesses all the eclectic ease that makes this look so appealing, and with a fresh feeling that is a delight to live with.

The country kitchen is an eternally popular look – cosy, welcoming and the perfect backdrop for an array of antique and vintage treasures. It works well in almost any home, too – big or small, urban or rural.

First and foremost, country-style kitchens shouldn't look too fitted. Plenty of storage and sufficient prep areas are important, but bland MDF/particleboard cabinets or laminated work surfaces are best avoided, if possible. Ideally, built-in cabinetry should be natural or painted wood which, while more expensive initially, looks beautiful and has longevity, not least because it can be sanded or repainted.

To add to this, turn to free-standing antique and vintage pieces. The key element in many a country kitchen is an old dresser/hutch adorned with rows of blue-and-white china, fresh flowers and all kinds of cherished bits and pieces. Glazed or mesh-fronted cabinets can be repurposed as pantry cupboards – trying painting them a bold colour (or just painting the inside) to create a stand-out piece. Open cabinets also look sweet with a gathered curtain to conceal their contents. Wall shelves can be an ideal solution if you're short of space, holding rows of pans, enamel storage jars or piled-up tableware, and bringing an easy-going country vibe. In terms of workspace, a butcher's block is a great alternative to a kitchen island, as is a free-standing farmhouse table.

Dressing the country kitchen is a joy. It's the perfect home for pretty, mismatched china and glassware found in charity shops/thrift stores and markets. Baskets (wire or wicker) work well as ad hoc storage. And have fun on the walls – vintage food posters look right, as do car boot/garage sale paintings and an old-fashioned clock.

Within a restrained colour palette, this kitchen attains a sumptuous mix of textures that makes the room feel both homely and luxurious. An inviting combination of old and new pieces includes a French shop sign, an array of bowls, plates and jugs, lovely worn chopping boards and antique linen tea towels.

LEFT An antique oak table and benches provide the perfect counterpoint to a run of smooth-fronted, handleless modern cabinets and a polished-concrete floor. Introducing rustic pieces like this can warm up a kitchen that has an otherwise streamlined, modern aesthetic.

BELOW LEFT This display of white-on-white includes the kinds of pretty ceramics and textiles that can be found relatively easily at antiques markets or online retailers and auctions. Keep the look pure and simple or, as here, introduce just a dash of colour as a contrast.

BELOW Look out for antique work benches or butcher's blocks. Their less-than-perfect lines and interesting surface textures will balance the more 'fitted' look of most modern kitchens, and they can provide useful storage, too. Unlike fitted kitchens, you can take them with you when you go.

OPPOSITE With low timber beams that make a strong statement, this pretty, cottagey dining room has been kept relatively simple, with a pale colour scheme, Gustavian-style dining chairs and a pretty, symmetrical display that includes a pair of traditional blue-and-white porcelain jars.

OPPOSITE A set of old shelves set on top of a vintage sideboard/credenza together provide a huge amount of storage for items both large and small in this unfitted kitchen. The Victorian-style drying rack, which operates via a ceiling-mounted pulley system, is a nostalgic touch, but can be a very practical addition to modern kitchens.

ABOVE Rows of ceramic and wooden plates, as well as some beautiful jugs, make a magnificent display on this old pine dresser, with antique crates below providing brilliant storage.

RIGHT A painted plaster bull stands guard over this charming pantry, with its open shelving and rows of glassware. Using a length of hemmed and gathered fabric to disguise open storage is an easy and inexpensive solution, informal and pretty, in this type of space.

Glorious colour

It's all too easy to see antiques or secondhand pieces as a collection of boring brown furniture. But there are many ways in which to inject luscious colour while including vintage finds. Kitchens and dining rooms are ideal for this treatment: in living rooms, bedrooms and bathrooms you may want glamour or relaxation, but when you're cooking or eating you can afford a little over-the-top exuberance.

Kitchens and dining rooms can make a decorative statement just like other rooms in the house. Tonal schemes of one shade only are dramatic and enveloping, while a confident use of contrasting colours can be uplifting and dynamic. Strong colour on the walls, whether painted, panelled or tiled, makes a great backdrop for the bold outlines of large pieces of antique furniture, the sculptural shapes of retro pieces or a collection of practical accessories.

The obvious go-to for a dash of colour is a fabulous array of mid-century-modern furniture and light fittings – a set of such dining chairs, for example, will immediately set the tone for the room. Alternatively, you may come across inexpensive second-hand brown furniture – whether chairs or tables, cupboards or chests – which could be carefully painted to co-ordinate with your scheme. And even in a kitchen with nothing more than painted walls and simple furnishings, you can add eye-catching jolts of colour and pattern in the form of crockery, glassware, table linens and storage containers in pretty pastels or clear, bright shades.

A multi-coloured set of DSR side chairs, designed by Charles and Ray Eames, add a retro note to a bold dining room, complementing the two capacious painted cupboards and panelling.

OPPOSITE Egg-yolk yellow seems an appropriate shade to use in this Cape Cod cottage kitchen, a soft and warm accompaniment to the various vintage furnishings and antique ice box.

RIGHT A modern cooker makes an efficient addition to this eclectic kitchen, with its vibrant zellige tiles and oversized star lantern. Even the ceiling has been painted blue, while the casual addition of a yellow tea towel creates a delicious counterpoint.

BELOW An effective use of green paint and abundant plants make this LA dining room an entrancing place in which to eat and socialise. By contrast, the white Panton chairs, conceived by Verner Panton in 1959, are rather restrained.

BELOW RIGHT Against a backdrop of a yellow-painted, planked wall, all that's needed for informal cutlery storage is a selection of vintage stoneware marmalade jars.

OPPOSITE In the kitchen of this Regency townhouse, the colours of a striking floral block-printed wallpaper are picked up by the coral red-painted table and green cupboards. It may be unconventional, but it is a strong and joyful look that looks wonderful in the high-ceilinged room.

OPPOSITE These Model 31 chairs by Danish designer Kai Kristiansen were designed in 1956. Made from solid teak with velvet upholstery, they are comfortable and supportive, a timeless design that works in virtually any decorative scheme.

Mid-century modern

There's something very distinctive about furniture designed in the middle of the twentieth century. Not only does it possess classic good looks and timeless appeal, but it mixes effortlessly with modern furnishings and is perfectly in harmony with antiques. The kitchen/diner or dining room is an excellent place to incorporate such versatile pieces in your home.

Whether you're looking for sideboards or dining tables, chairs or shelving, mid-century modern makes a fabulous choice. Sadly, it's no longer common to stumble across unnoticed designer furniture from this period in jumble sales, skips/dumpsters or house clearances – its popularity means that prices are at a premium – but you can still source it through specialists and vintage marketplaces or auctions, both online and otherwise. Alternatively, some companies continue to manufacture pieces to the original designs, while others produce close copies that, to the non-purist, are just as appealing. There are, of course, also many mass-produced mid-century furnishings that are fabulously attractive. Even early IKEA pieces (it was founded in 1943) are becoming collectible.

To ensure that mid-century furnishings look their best, banish clutter and keep accessories to a minimum – lots of decorative bits and bobs are better suited to a country kitchen. Walls painted in neutral or strong yet sophisticated tones provide a calm backdrop for this style, as do simple wooden floors. Modern fitted kitchens can perfectly complement mid-century furniture, particularly if you pay attention to details such as handles and taps/faucets. Steer clear of panelled cabinetry with traditional knobs or handles, or anything remotely rustic.

Lighting was a preoccupation of many mid-century designers, so recessed spotlights, throwing light exactly where required, can be combined with table lamps on a sideboard, sculptural wall fittings, or pendants hung low over a dining table. You may wish to keep walls clean and clear, but a graphic 1950s poster or two (look on Etsy for originals and reproductions) would definitely strike the right tone.

ABOVE The Eames dining chair, affectionately known as the 'Eiffel chair' due to its metal base, is an instantly recognizable classic, fitting effortlessly into any style of room, whether rustic or urban, traditional or modern.

OPPOSITE In a glamorous dining room, the ornate, scrolling forms of a set of Hollywood Regency gold chairs from the 1950s contrasts with the blocky lines of a 1960s sideboard – and even more so with a large carved and gilded mirror frame.

ABOVE Charcoal-black cabinetry, an extraordinary marble splashback and old mahogany floorboards provide a luxurious and dramatic backdrop for a set of beautiful mid-century dining chairs and a 1950s Italian glass chandelier.

LEFT Charles and Ray Eames designed the DCW plywood chair in 1945, its organic shape and warm, natural wood inviting relaxation. This set looks particularly at home in a timber-clad dining room with its polished-concrete floor.

OPPOSITE This mid-century shelving unit is an ingenious way to partially divide a kitchen from a living room, providing both display space and storage while allowing light to pass from one area to the other.

LEFT Grouped around a matching dining table, these iconic 1950s Cherner chairs make a striking centrepiece in an modern kitchen with wooden floors and a stainless-steel splashback.

OPPOSITE The kitchen of this Oslo apartment has a glamorous mid-century feel, featuring a wall of cabinets in shades of pink as well as an island in green marble and brass. The stackable chairs were designed in 1977 by Börge Lindau and Bo Lindekrantz, while the table and chandelier are both vintage.

RIGHT Simply constructed, highly comfortable and very beautiful, the CH29 Sawbuck chair was originally designed for Carl Hansen & Søn by Hans Wegner in 1952. These elegant pieces have really stood the test of time; in this minimal dining space they look wonderful teamed with a classic PH 5 pendant light designed by Paul Henningsen for Louis Poulsen in 1958.

COOKING & EATING *Style guide*

- Combine and contrast textures for a feel that is inviting and individual: smooth, shiny stainless steel against rough, bare brickwork, or grained wood against soft wool upholstery, for example.

- Plan plenty of storage, but not necessarily in the form of fitted mass-produced modern cabinets. Old dressers/hutches, cupboards, butchers' blocks, trolleys and open shelves are all great additions to the mix.

- Modern kitchens tend to be square and hard-edged. If this look doesn't suit you, add furniture with curvy outlines (such as old Parisian café chairs or even just one comfy old armchair) or items that are softer and more giving – perhaps an antique kilim under a dining table, or a pair of pretty 1950s floral-print curtains.

- If you're on a tight budget, a set of dining chairs can represent a considerable outlay. Instead of heading for mass-produced furniture outlets, take a look at online marketplaces. Old chapel chairs are sturdy and good looking, as are solid wood slat-back farmhouse-style chairs, while curvy mid-century styles are lightweight and versatile. And an old bench seats many people and can be pushed under the table when not in use.

- Everyone loves showing off their antique and vintage finds, but be disciplined when it comes to open shelves and surfaces. Having too many small items on display is never as effective as a few carefully chosen pieces. One huge antique wooden bowl full of fruit will have much more impact than lots of smaller bits and pieces.

- Bear in mind that the heights of old and new chairs and dining tables may not match up – take measurements carefully before you rush into making a purchase.

- Old cupboards and dressers/hutches can sometimes be improved by changing the knobs or handles, or by replacing cracked or warped door panels with fabric or glass. A coat of paint can also give new life to items – look for chalk paint as it comes in a rainbow of colours and doesn't require much preparation.

OPPOSITE An elegant mix of beautiful antiques and vintage pieces creates a bedroom that's a calm oasis. The Chinoiserie wallpaper picks up on the leafy view from the window and provides a sophisticated backdrop to the furnishings, which include a lovely antique chest of drawers/dresser, a 1950s-style wall light and a mid-century-inspired table lamp.

SLEEPING

Decorating the private space of one's bedroom allows for a personal and creative approach. It's the perfect home for treasured antique or vintage pieces – perhaps items handed down by family members or that are too delicate to be used by everyone in the household. For a harmonious mix look for furnishings that complement each other in terms of shape and colour, creating a feeling of comfort, rest and relaxation.

RIGHT A laid-back feel is key to the inviting ambience of this 19th-century cottage in Cape Cod. The cream and gold wallpaper is vintage, as is the iron bed frame, which was bought from an online auction site and left in its delightfully distressed state. A simple lamp and white-painted side table complete the look.

OPPOSITE A mix of Scandinavian-style, rustic and vintage furnishings combine seamlessly against a backdrop of white walls in the bedroom of this coastal home. The crisp, dark armoire makes a dramatic counterpoint to the white linens and other natural textures.

Calm and cosy

For a bedroom that's a calming sanctuary offering respite from busy daily life, use antiques to create an atmosphere that's restful and relaxed.

In bedrooms large or small you can combine modern comforts with a sprinkling of antique or vintage pieces to create an inviting feel and a sense of tranquillity. Lots of hardworking storage is absolutely key to a calm and uncluttered atmosphere, and this is where freestanding antique or vintage furnishings come into their own – consider a roomy armoire, linen press or chest of drawers/dresser (such pieces are often surprisingly good value as well as sturdy and long-lived). If dark wood is not your style, pieces can be stripped or sanded then painted with milk paint or white wax.

The bed is, of course, another key item. A modern divan is practical and may have the benefit of a storage drawer underneath, but an antique bed teamed with a new mattress will be prettier. Old iron beds, for example, are timeless and sturdy, and provide a welcome note of decorative detail. Sleigh beds and four-posters are also good choices, while a modern bed could, potentially, be teamed with an old headboard to add character.

Also essential in a room devoted to calm and relaxation are effective window treatments. To achieve maximum darkness with no draughts, opt for lined curtains or blinds/shades in heavy linen or wool, perhaps trimmed with antique braid or lace. Cotton ticking is smart yet understated, and relatively inexpensive. Early risers may prefer sheers, while vintage linen tray cloths or French tablecloths can be fashioned into unlined, cafe-style curtains that cover the bottom part of the window for privacy during the daytime. To dress the bed, look to textiles in pale, co-ordinating colours – perhaps a vintage matelasse coverlet, satin-edged blanket or lacy crochet throw, and add an artwork or two for a personal touch.

OPPOSITE The restricted tonal palette of this tranquil bedroom creates a warm and welcoming vibe. The vintage painting is a focal point, its colours providing inspiration for the rest of the room.

RIGHT Natural textures and neutral colours set the tone of this room. The wavy form of the moulded-plywood screen by Charles and Ray Eames is underlined by that of the 1950s chaise longue, designed by Edward Wormley. Wood-panelled walls add to the sense of refined yet understated luxury.

LEFT The walls of this bedroom are painted in a restful shade of eco-paint, which has a slightly textured finish. Rumpled bed linen and an old side table are all that's necessary for simple comfort – nothing extra needed.

PAGE 84 An antique four-poster bed always forms the focal point of a bedroom. This example needs nothing more than white linen and a faux-fur throw to create a simple yet luxurious look. The wooden wall panel used to be covered in mirrored tiles, which have left behind an intriguing pattern.

PAGE 85 In this 18th-century family home, stripped-back walls reveal centuries of layered paintwork – just as good as any work of art. Alongside a vintage side table sits a low bedroom chair, given a new lease of life with interesting upholstery.

AFRICA
Richard Dowden

OPPOSITE The appeal of this shabby-chic bedroom is all in the layering of appealing textiles. Gingham, florals and a pretty quilt are piled atop a Victorian-style metal bed. Natural textures in the form of weathered wood and a soft rug contribute to the homely yet pretty vibe.

RIGHT Cleverly combining the same pink and red shades, these textiles combine different florals beautifully. The quilting and the gilded wood add to the sumptuous and inviting effect.

A touch of romance

There'll always be those of us who can't resist the opulence of an ultra-romantic bedroom, one that possesses comfort and glamour in equal measure.

Romantic bedrooms are the ideal setting for a magnificent antique or vintage bed – a one-off purchase that makes a bold statement and captivates the eye. There are many options to choose from – a four-poster, a French bergere style with caned panels or a wooden sleigh bed – but what's important is that it has a sumptuous, indulgent feel. Add a chaise longue or a slipper chair, an oversized gilt mirror or a pretty French dressing table – all or any of these pieces will contribute to an evocative atmosphere.

In terms of colour, choose pinks, lilacs and soft blues or go for rich, glamorous burnished golds and bronzes, and remember that texture is important, too. Soft wools (or even cashmere), deep upholstery, lace, tassels and fringing can all play a part. Another way to bring charm to a bedroom is via tactile textiles – floral fabrics, vintage quilts or faded satin eiderdowns. Don't hold back: you need layer upon layer to make he room look the part.

To complete the mood of comfort, include lighting that can be adjusted to provide a gentle ambiance when necessary. A twinkling chandelier, beaded pendant or pair of gilt wall sconces, combined with elegant bedside lamps, will do the trick. Finally, add a generous layer of accessories. Needlepoint cushions hit the right note, as would a velvet throw, tactile rug or Victorian cut-glass scent bottle. Hang pictures and mirrors on the walls or prop them on the floor, and don't forget a simple vase of seasonal flowers.

RIGHT Use vintage florals as the basis for a simple and pretty guest bedroom. Here, a dark wooden bed frame has been painted chalky white and teamed with a floral bedspread. The finishing touch is an armful of hydrangeas in an old enamel bucket.

BELOW The textural combinations in this room, from exposed old beams to ribbed sisal, are simply irresistible. Cream upholstery on a vintage bed is the perfect foil for blue and teal bedding, accentuated by a green adjustable lamp on the old chest of drawers/dresser.

BELOW RIGHT Deeply buttoned/tufted upholstery always adds a touch of opulence. This chaise longue is enhanced by a plump eiderdown with a ruffled edge.

OPPOSITE When sourcing antique and vintage furniture, look for pieces that are solid and well made, with an attractive grain and a pleasing colour. This sturdy sleigh bed is a fabulous example of enduring quality.

OPPOSITE & BELOW This Victorian coastal house is furnished almost entirely with vintage pieces, and the bay-windowed bedroom is no different, its centrepiece a shell bed that was a lucky junk-shop find. It is set against a backdrop of hand-painted coral murals outlined in thousands of real, glued-on shells, a pair of reupholstered boudoir-style armchairs with deep buttoning/tufting and fringing, a low-hung, boho chandelier and a taxidermy swan. Despite its undoubted eccentricities, the room feels calm and welcoming.

OPPOSITE A hand-painted botanical
mural creates an all-embracing backdrop
in this bedroom, complementing
curtains made from antique velvet
bought from a market stall, an ornate
metal bed and an antique tea table.

Understated elegance

If frills and flourishes arent your style, look to elegant, dignified antique
and vintage pieces to create a bedroom that's handsome and refined.

To put together this look, the emphasis is not placed on one statement item, but rather on carefully chosen furniture and accessories that blend into a seamless whole. The bed could be relatively plain, and dressed with tailored linens in serene shades or simple patterns. Accentuate a sense of luxury by adding rugs with subtle pattern or interesting textures; you could even hang a rug or other textiles on the wall for an enveloping effect.

Perhaps the most important creator of mood is colour. Naturals and neutrals – off-white, taupe, stone, shell and so on – will offset dark antiques. Alternatively, choose deeper, more subdued shades, from charcoal to navy, for a calm and cocooning atmosphere. Classic wallpapers are another way to add atmosphere and complement elegant antiques: Chinoiserie, William Morris and toile de Jouy, for example, would all work well.

In general, keep furnishings to a minimum, with each piece chosen expressly for its quality of materials and manufacture. Classic Scandinavian modern pieces are ideal, with their emphasis on function as well as aesthetics. Alternatively, look for sober and elegant 19th-century furniture: a wardrobe or armoire, bedside table/nightstand, bedroom chair, tallboy or chest of drawers, perhaps a folding screen to hide a dressing area or a cheval glass instead of a wall mirror.

Getting the lighting right is vital. Recessed downlighters will provide general illumination, while understated vintage wall or table lamps can provide more targeted light where necessary while contributing to the overall scheme in terms of shape, size and material. Complete the effect with displays of personal treasures, such as framed paintings or family photographs, favourite books or scented candles.

PAGES 94–95 Plain, earthy colours provide an utter sense of tranquillity in this attic bedroom. Crisp, straight lines (including those of the picture frames and the window) are complemented by the softer shapes of the mid-century Butterfly chair and the vintage rattan armchair.

ABOVE LEFT An antique or vintage chair can provide a beautiful accent of colour, shape, pattern or texture in a bedroom. Here, a Model 31 chair by Kai Kristiansen, designed in 1956, complements a teak sideboard and a vintage brass wall sconce.

ABOVE RIGHT The classic English manor-house look in this guest bedroom is achieved with a combination of old furnishings against a backdrop of hand-painted Chinese wallpaper and pink-painted cupboards. Above the fireplace hangs a Regency convex mirror.

OPPOSITE Against a large-scale neo-classical *trompe l'oeil* mural, a brass bed with a gathered-linen valance and faux-fur throw is accompanied by a Louis XVI chair – used as a handy bedside surface – and a versatile tilt-top table.

SLEEPING *Style guide*

- Avoid bedroom clutter by investing in spacious, handsome and well-made antique wardrobes/armoires, cupboards and chests of drawers/dressers. Reclaimed shop fittings like vintage haberdashery counters have quirky appeal and, if you have a wall of built-in storage, one interesting piece will add character.

- The bed should be the focal point of the room. If you can afford a beautiful antique style, keep the linen simple and understated, so the bed's design can really stand out. Old metal beds dating from Victorian times and onwards are easy to track down; for a more eclectic mood, they can be spray-painted in bold shades such as orange, teal or leaf green.

- A clever colour scheme can pull the whole look together, uniting antique and modern pieces seamlessly. Generally, pale colours such as ivory and taupe are calming and restful, but stronger, deeper colours can be more cosy and inviting.

- Keep flooring neutral – you want a plain backdrop that shows off furniture with interesting shapes to its best advantage.

- A bedside rug is wonderfully comforting first thing in the morning. Old Oriental rugs or kelims are soft underfoot after years of use and can add subtle pattern to a room.

- Even if you invest in a wonderful antique bed, you should always buy a good-quality new mattress. We spend an average of twenty-five years of our lives in bed, so it's worth ensuring it's not lumpy, too hard or too soft.

- Choose solidly made furniture that works together by virtue of colour, shape or material. The less fussy the decoration and the cleaner the lines, the more likely that old and new pieces will harmonize well.

- • Accessories can provide interesting touches in a bedroom scheme, from enamel jugs to chintz-printed bowls, vintage quilts to sunburst mirrors, milking stools to tailor's dummies. Just ensure that you don't overfill the room with too much stuff. Instead, choose pieces that contribute to the overall look and provide a balance with other furnishings.

- A bedside lamp is an essential, whether it's a classic 1970s task lamp or a vintage ceramic base paired with a new shade. Etsy and eBay are good places to search for vintage lamp bases but make sure they have been tested to meet modern regulations.

- Don't forget a full-length mirror — a freestanding antique or vintage cheval glass is an elegant solution.

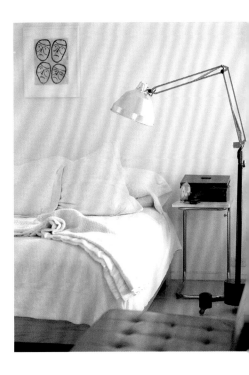

This superb freestanding bathtub was a bargain from an online auction site – it simply needed new taps and a coat of black paint. The worn wooden bench and overmantel mirror were both vintage finds, too.

BATHING

Modern bathrooms can be quite clinical spaces, so adding antique or vintage furnishings, artworks or accessories can offset hard edges and shiny finishes to create a sense of welcome and individuality. Interesting juxtapositions, such as modern brassware with a vintage or reclaimed roll-top bathtub, promote a sense of drama, while an understated scheme provides a chance to unwind in calm surroundings.

OPPOSITE Create a peaceful escape using soft colours and natural textures, as in this wonderfully restful bathroom. The walls are painted a gentle dusty pink, which has a historical resonance yet also feels fresh and contemporary. White-painted floorboards make the room feel light and bright, while the 1930s chair, together with the flatweave rug and shell print, soften the look overall.

RIGHT For bathroom indulgence, a deep ceramic sink is both practical and beautiful. It is relatively straightforward to mount a basin on a reclaimed or upcycled cabinet, providing convenient storage and display space for toiletries.

Spa sanctuary

For a bathroom that's a tranquil and indulgent escape, introduce interesting antique and vintage shapes and a variety of appealing textures.

Central to this look is a really comfortable bathtub – if possible one that's slightly larger than average and, maybe, if you're lucky, freestanding. An original Edwardian roll-top tub with claw feet would be ideal, while an ordinary built-in tub can be made more interesting with the addition of a side panel, perhaps in reclaimed timber or covered with charming vintage tiles.

For an intriguing contrast, combine an old bath or sink with streamlined modern taps/faucets and shower attachments. A similar effect can be achieved by setting a modern sink on a stripped-pine washstand or below an antique Venetian or foxed mirror.

In general, try to avoid too much uniform tiling on the walls, which can give a sterile and chilly feel to a room – a good alternative is panelling painted in a muted heritage shade. Make a home for your towels and cleaning products in an antique chest of drawers or cupboard, and stash toiletries in a glazed wall cabinet, on a wall-mounted shelf or perhaps a retro drinks trolley.

Finally, add a vintage chair or stool to hold discarded clothes, books and the like, a soft flatweave rug, some wall art and a plant or two. The overall effect should be light and airy or soft and subtle, to create as peaceful and inviting an atmosphere as possible.

ABOVE This reproduction slipper bathtub has been painted off-black and given additional drama by raising it on a plinth of black-and-white Moroccan tiles. The shower was created out of a variety of old brass plumbing parts, with its rose formed by punching holes in a piece of brass for a rain-like spray.

ABOVE RIGHT In this serene bathroom, a modern, freestanding tub and a sleek pendant lamp are complemented by a huge antique mirror and vintage factory stool.

OPPOSITE A decorative wrought-iron trolley offers useful storage in this bright, pared-back bathroom. The roll-top, claw-foot bathtub is teamed with a sturdy 1930s pedestal basin and an opulent Venetian-glass mirror, its scrolling shapes echoing those of the trolley's metalwork.

ABOVE LEFT This huge, square tub is sharp and modern, its effect tempered by the watery-pale tiles and a pair of vintage cross-head taps/faucets with a gently worn patina.

ABOVE An old-school peg rail shelf can be repurposed almost anywhere in the house. In a pure white bathroom it adds colour and texture, while providing hanging and display space for all kinds of useful things.

LEFT The pair of carvings placed symmetrically in a triangular chimney breast are the focal point of this bathroom. The plain wall provides an understated backdrop for the ornate fireplace and traditional taps/faucets.

OPPOSITE The purity of the wet room in this Danish weekend house is achieved by its expanse of dark, smooth yet subtly textured surfaces. The vintage rustic milking stool makes a perfect counterpoint.

RIGHT & OPPOSITE This handsome room makes a big impression. Glossy, dark wall tiles with a leafy motif, ornate fixtures and brass fittings are complemented by touches of warm wood and a fabulous etched-glass mirror. The chequered flooring brings a contrasting pattern in black and white, which harmonizes with the bold palette.

Statement suites

If your home is a dramatic space, why should the bathroom to be any different? Use antiques or one-off vintage pieces to make a statement and delight the eye.

The secret to achieving the wow factor is one showstopping feature, whether it's an unusual bathtub, a reclaimed tile splashback or an impressive mirror. Specialists in antique sanitaryware sometimes have amazing copper tubs, reclaimed brass shower heads and Art Deco sinks in pastel colours, but they don't come cheap. A less expensive alternative is to use plain fittings and combine them with bold paint colours and interesting freestanding pieces, be these old chairs, side tables, chests or cabinets.

Another way of making a statement is with a large pedestal basin (or even a double basin for added wow factor) or a bathroom sink mounted onto an antique commode or chest of drawers, to create a vanity unit that offers a dramatic contrast of smooth ceramic or gleaming metal with dark, grained wood.

Because this look is intended to be maximalist, hunt for pieces with elaborate, decorative shapes and forms – bring on the gilt mirrors, the carved furniture and antique wall lights. For a unified look, however, keep to a coherent colour scheme, and make sure that your furnishings show a similar decorative intent, even if they come from different time periods.

OPPOSITE Despite its vintage appearance, this enormous tin tub is actually modern. Its gently polished surface is a lovely foil to the sleek, smooth look of the glass wall and minimal floor-mounted tap/faucet, while the antique mirror adds another interesting patina.

ABOVE These vintage mirrors add dashing retro glamour, complementing the extravagant chandelier (seen reflected) and curvy double vanity. The ochre walls are warm and tranquil, and make a wonderful contrast to both the creamy sanitaryware and the shiny metallics.

ABOVE The patina of a copper bathtub contrasts with that of an antique Chinese cabinet in this New York brownstone bathroom.

RIGHT A high-sided copper tub always makes a statement, and in this room its warm lustre is contrasted with the rougher textures of rugged stonework.

OPPOSITE With two shaped shelves, this unusual wooden vanity with turned supports is a practical addition to a black-and-white shower room. Just as importantly, it adds interest, bringing in the warmth and grain of natural wood and a sense of history that is utterly unique.

The warm tone of an antique mahogany wall cupboard adds richness to this eclectic bathroom with its pair of surface-mounted ceramic basins. The vintage brass ship's lights are a lovely touch. In general, lighting designed to be used outdoors will satisfy most electric regulations in a bathroom, so is worth investigating.

LEFT Let worn, used textures speak for themselves. In this Danish home, a zinc bucket makes a great basin. It has been plumbed into an old wooden industrial unit that handily provides shelving beneath.

BELOW Clever contrasts in texture create a sense of drama in this intriguing bathroom. Smooth stone panelling meets rough concrete on the walls, while a weathered zinc tub complements a brass tap/faucet, a gilt-framed mirror and tactile accessories.

BELOW When space allows, adding a side table to a bathroom is a lovely idea, offering a chance to introduce some vintage magic as well as additional storage or a display area. This antique shaving stand is illuminated by a reclaimed swan-neck factory wall light.

OPPOSITE A country-style interior can avoid the wall-to-wall tiling and unobtrusive lighting that is typical of many modern bathrooms in favour of decor that looks much more like any traditional room – including floorboards and pretty pendants. Adding vintage pieces such as a cupboard, chest of drawers/dresser or chair adds to the pleasing mix of materials and overall sense of informality.

RIGHT Mounted on a vintage chest of drawers/dresser, this ceramic sink has both traditional good looks and sturdy practicality. The tiles behind are zellige, handmade in natural clay and with a unique, irregular finish that simply adds to their charm.

Country classic

The country-style bathroom is simple and functional, uncomplicated and unpretentious, with a leisurely yet slightly utilitarian feel. It offers a welcome retreat from modern life – somewhere simple and pretty to relax and unwind.

Natural materials are at the heart of this look, and most essential of all is wood. Tongue-and-groove wall panelling adds a rustic flavour while providing a practical wall covering, especially when coated with paint specially formulated for bathrooms. Stripped floorboards also strike the right note, although in a cooler climate you might want to scatter a few rag rugs or vintage runners underfoot.

If possible, try to avoid the uniform, glossy-white sleekness of modern, fitted sanitaryware. Roll-top bathtubs look just right, and if you've inherited clinical modern fittings, these can be combined with freestanding wooden furnishing such as chests of drawers, benches and glass-fronted cupboards. You could create an unfitted mood by plumbing an old washstand with a countertop basin, perhaps also teamed with reclaimed and restored taps/faucets.

Vintage accessories in modest and unassuming materials, such as enamelled buckets and wicker baskets, will help to contribute to an effect of simple, uncontrived rusticity. Add yet more old-fashioned charm in the form of antique mirrors, some plants in pretty pots, a linen or cotton ticking shower curtain, a wooden wall shelf and a stool beside the bath to hold a scented candle or a glass of wine.

ABOVE There is no substitute for a freestanding, claw-foot tub when creating a traditional look in a bathroom. Accessories such as works of art, rugs and even a wooden bath bridge all add to the effect, even when the background is plain and simple.

ABOVE RIGHT Distressed timber planks provide a unique and interesting alternative to wall tiles, combined with a beautiful old basin with an integral shelf. A metal cabinet has been repurposed for storage, with an enamel bucket as a bin/trashcan.

OPPOSITE Old and new mix very easily in this coastal townhouse, which was renovated on a budget and includes a variety of reclaimed finds and hand-made pieces. A pair of vintage shell lamps adorn the wall above a minimal basin, but the undoubted star is the lavish shower curtain made from an old lace-trimmed linen bedsheet.

BATHING
Style guide

- Adding freestanding pieces (low chairs, stools, benches, chests, trolleys or large plants) is a good way to break out of the boring fitted-bathroom mould.

- Antique lighting may not be suitable for bathrooms, but an ornate mirror will reflect light around the room and draw attention away from modern light fittings.

- Remember that the spaces in between are as important as the furnishings themselves. An old-fashioned washstand with a metal frame allows more of the floor space to be visible, creating a spacious, airy feel.

- If you are on a budget, look out for interesting pieces of furniture and pretty accessories in markets, junk and antique shops that will stand out against affordable modern fittings, adding balance and colour.

- If necessary, you can have old bathtubs re-enamelled so that their surfaces are clean, new and comfortable to bathe in.

- When buying old bathroom fittings, it's important to check that all the dimensions will correspond with modern plumbing.

- If you are thinking of installing a large reclaimed cast-iron bathtub, first make sure that your floor is strong enough to support the combined weight of the tub, the water and a bather – a substantial load. Check with a structural engineer if in any doubt.

- Source reclaimed vintage tiles, which possess gorgeous colours and patterns, to introduce unique character over small areas such as a basin splashback.

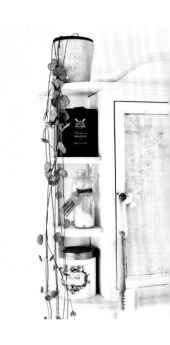

THE
ELEMENTS

OPPOSITE This shabby-chic painted bench sits prettily on a reclaimed brick floor in a 17th-century Suffolk cottage, where it is teamed with a sturdy table. Both are wonderful examples of how antique furniture can enhance a room.

FURNITURE

Carefully chosen antique and vintage furnishings of all kinds combine beauty with practicality. Why not place a simple farm stool in a bedroom, use a former factory locker for storage in the kitchen or add a comfortable 1930s chair to a corner of the living room? Whether a prized, unusual item or an everyday, functional piece, their unique character is an inspiring addition to any home.

Seating

From a cast-iron garden bench to a 1960s bent-ply dining chair, antique and vintage seating comes in all shapes and sizes, is full of impact, and need not be expensive. You may opt for a statement piece by a well-known designer, or scour auctions and markets for cheaper options that blend in without fuss. And if an old seat is a little battered or tired, it can, without great difficulty be brought back to life. That second-hand wooden dining chair can be sanded, painted, stained, varnished or re-caned, while sagging sofas and chairs may be re-upholstered or re-covered using cotton, canvas or velvet to complement most schemes.

What style are you looking for? Leather club chairs or 1930s Lloyd Loom chairs add a note of old-fashioned comfort, for example, while Louis-style carved wooden benches are classically elegant and mid-century modern pieces add a note of chic sophistication. Interesting seating, of whatever type, is a great place to start when creating your personal look.

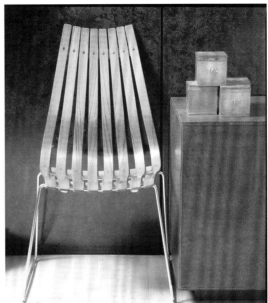

OPPOSITE A Donald Judd-style daybed in natural wood sits in opposition to a white leather Barcelona chair by Ludwig Mies van der Rohe. They were designed around 50 years apart, yet their simple, spare lines and high quality ensure they work in harmony with each other.

TOP LEFT A comfortable club chair in burnished leather is perfectly at home in a room with stripped floorboards and plain white walls.

TOP RIGHT The widely imitated stackable Scandia chair was designed by Hans Brattrud in 1957. Made from laminated wood on a pliable wire frame, its shape and style have definitely stood the test of time.

ABOVE LEFT Simple lines and a pared-down form ensure that this Eames chair sits naturally in a contemporary living room.

ABOVE RIGHT The Barcelona chair, designed in 1929, is now a modern classic, at home in any style of interior. This matching pair is seen reflected in the mirror behind.

ABOVE Look out for iron garden chairs, usually French and dating to the early 20th century, which can make a pretty addition to an indoor space. This example contrasts nicely with a Tulip stool by Eero Saarinen, designed in 1957.

ABOVE RIGHT In this 19th-century home, an antique daybed makes a beautiful complement to the old, beaded walls. The indigo and cream cushion covers were made from old linens.

OPPOSITE Antique armchairs are often constructed sturdily, using handmade joints and high-quality timber. Even if the fabric has deteriorated, they are well worth the investment, and replacement upholstery will give them a new lease of life. Classic styles such as these will look superb in any room.

LEFT The many small drawers of a vintage apothecary cabinet have multiple possible uses – even including plant displays. This gorgeous example is dramatically juxtaposed with a Stendig wall calendar, created by the legendary Italian designer Massimo Vignelli in 1966.

OPPOSITE This vintage metal tallboy would not look out of place in the corner of a factory. It also makes a useful and stylish addition to a sitting room, with banks of drawers and a lovely worn patina.

Storage

Every home needs plenty of storage (can we ever have enough?), and old pieces offer a clever way to blend practicality with aesthetic appeal. Vintage chests, cabinets, dressers/hutches, wardrobes, armoires and sideboards/credenzas can play a useful role in daily life while also making an invaluable contribution to your decorative scheme.

All kinds of special period pieces, from a 19th-century Italian wardrobe to a lacquered Chinese cabinet, can add impact to a room, while humbler vintage storage furniture can be adapted to modern usage, perhaps in unexpected ways. A 1940s polished-steel filing cabinet could be a quirky place to keep toiletries in a bathroom, while a carved-oak coffer might hold umbrellas in a hallway and a farmhouse dresser/hutch could be a new home for a record player or TV. Seek out interesting items, be willing to experiment and your imaginative approach will reap rewards.

In an airy, modern room, the beautiful grain of an old wooden plan chest adds character and individuality. Its large surface also offers the chance to create attractive displays.

OPPOSITE A fabulous mirrored armoire has moved from the bedroom to the living room, where it now serves as a striking and unusual drinks cabinet.

RIGHT Wall shelves with dividers are incredibly versatile and can be put to good use almost anywhere. Use them for books, vases, scented candles, small plants, stacks of bowls or, as here, a tonally arranged display of bottles and jars.

BELOW An exquisite piece, this antique gilt commode really sings out against the simple background of white walls and black floorboards. Its sophistication makes a nice juxtaposition with rustic wooden beams.

BELOW RIGHT The utilitarian nature of this vintage sideboard complements that of the old work stool next to it.

OPPOSITE A dark and somewhat monumental commode provides plenty of storage in the study of this London apartment, balanced by an acrylic-and-steel chair from the 1970s and a modern glass-topped desk.

OPPOSITE A rustic table can set the tone for a country-style dining room or provide a welcome textural contrast in a more urban setting. This example is surrounded by a set of Antelope chairs, designed by Ernest Race for the Festival of Britain in 1951, which adds more interest in terms of shape, material and colour.

RIGHT With traditional construction joints and A-frame legs, this rustic wooden 'pig' bench would once have been found on a farm or smallholding. Today, it makes a sweet spot on which to place a simple vase filled with greenery.

Tables

An antique or vintage table will always make an impression while adding functionality to a room, whether it's a large dining table around which to gather with friends or a tiny side table just right for holding a book and a mug of coffee.

One of the most exciting opportunities for interesting juxtapositions of styles and periods is offered by a dining table and its surrounding chairs. Contrast the strength and solidity of a scrubbed-pine farmhouse table with chairs in smooth plywood, glossy plastic or sleek steel. Alternatively, combine a mid-century table with old school chairs or dark-wood antiques. The chairs don't have to match – seek out attractive examples in markets, junk shops or even skips/dumpsters.

Side tables, console tables, bedside tables and coffee tables can also be essential elements. A huge coffee table made from reclaimed railway sleepers/railroad ties or an old Indian door would look fabulous in a minimal living room, while a vintage Formica plant stand could be a neat addition to a traditional hallway.

LEFT Said to have been a favourite of Coco Chanel, wheatsheaf tables were popular in the mid 20th century and still add a welcome touch of glamour, with a glass top that makes them highly practical, too.

BELOW Vintage garden furniture can suit a conservatory or room with an indoor/outdoor feel, and this pretty set has a touch of vintage style that gives added interest. It may be possible to pick up sets relatively cheaply, but do check for signs of rust – unless you wish to make a feature of a distressed finish.

OPPOSITE A rich diversity of antique side tables can be sourced from shops, markets and online, for use in all kinds of settings. This example has an interesting tripod base, an unusual shape and a gorgeous polished finish, making it an eye-catching feature in itself, as well as a useful surface on which to display a piece of sculpture.

OPPOSITE A pair of salvaged factory pendants with bright blue flexes provides an attractive counterpoint to the pale-pink walls of this dining room. Replacing an old plastic flex with a coloured cotton one is a lovely touch and a straightforward upgrade to many vintage lights.

LIGHTING

When you're looking for illumination that makes a statement, antique or vintage is the answer. Nothing beats the brilliance of a crystal chandelier, the eye-catching dynamism of a mid-century table lamp or the drama of an oversized industrial pendant. Check for compliance with modern safety regulations, then enhance your room with antique lighting that adds instant appeal.

OPPOSITE As bedside illumination goes, hanging a small, tiered chandelier is an inspired idea. Its pretty twinkle makes a delightful contrast to the weathered timber headboard, and it possesses truly timeless charm.

RIGHT Make a statement with a large, swing-arm wall lamp that is as much a work of art as a lighting piece. This fabulous example was designed by Serge Mouille in 1954.

Ceiling and wall lights

For a touch of glamour in almost any room, an antique chandelier is the obvious choice. They range in style from relatively simple to extremely ornate, and prices vary greatly, too, though it is still possible to find affordable examples. But they're not the only option when it comes to ceiling lights. Why not try a trio of old factory lamps over a dining table, a rise-and-fall Holophane glass fitting above a kitchen island or a Scandinavian retro pendant in the living room?

Mid-century modern lighting is hugely influential these days, and vintage pendant fittings by, or in the style of, masters of their art such as Serge Mouille, Poul Henningsen and Gaetano Sciolari, will introduce sleek, minimal lines and a refreshing, retro spirit to your interior scheme.

As for wall lamps, you might choose anything from a pair of crystal and gilt sconces in the bedroom to a swing-arm brass reading light in the study. Positioned for maximum impact, such pieces will always dazzle and delight.

ABOVE LEFT This bentwood pendant has a definite vintage feel. Its simple shape and lovely patina would complement most rooms.

ABOVE RIGHT Rise-and-fall pendants were popular during the late 19th century, when they were often used above dressing tables in the bedroom or a table in the living room. Today, we are more likely to install one over a kitchen island or a dining table. This is a crimped-edge, opaline glass version in a 'pie-crust' style that is particularly suitable for country cottages and period homes.

BELOW LEFT Elaborate in style and very pretty, this chandelier includes both teardrop and cut-glass droplets in varying sizes for maximum impact.

BELOW RIGHT Antique glass looks striking when juxtaposed with contemporary furnishings. Even a small wall lamp will draw the eye with an element of sparkle.

OPPOSITE Oversized lamps salvaged from factories make a big impression when hung low over a dining table. They combine a strong sense of history and personality with practical function.

LEFT The Arco floor lamp was designed by Achille and Pier Castiglioni in 1962. With a heavy marble base and a swivelling, height-adjustable stem, it can bring overhead light to any area of the room, and is now an icon of modern design.

OPPOSITE Adding a tall tripod base to a large vintage industrial light – such as a searchlight, theatre projector or railway light – results in a fascinating piece of history that is as useable as it is attractive.

Floor and table lamps

Unlike wired-in ceiling and wall lights, antique floor and table lamps are easy to install – just plug in and you're done. For added versatility, they can also be moved around whenever and wherever you wish, illuminating dark corners and creating points of decorative interest.

One of the more readily available types of vintage lamp is an articulated-arm desk lamp, the best known of which are Anglepoise and Jieldé. These metal lamps are, of course, perfect for home offices, but work equally well in spaces from the living room to the bedroom. Plenty more styles of both table and floor fitting can also be found, ranging from coloured-glass Tiffany lamps to bold 1960s plastics. While iconic pieces by well-known names command premium prices, it is worth spending time seeking out quality pieces by lesser-known or anonymous designers and brands. With a little effort you will come across all kinds of intriguing table and floor lights that will, without great expense, enliven any room.

The Trixel table lamp was created for Lyfa by Danish architect-designer Bent Karlby in the 1960s. Made from Perspex and brass, it has a 'space age' look that is typical of the time and, in this home office, complements the curves of the 1959 Panton chair perfectly.

LEFT & BELOW Vintage or pre-loved table lamps from all periods make a wonderful decorative feature. They can easily be given new shades if necessary or if preferred.

BELOW LEFT The Jieldé Loft two-arm desk light is a good-looking and popular example of the industrial work lamps frequently produced in the 1950s. The brand was established by mechanic Jean-Louis Domecq, who designed the range after being unable to find lighting suitable for his work.

OPPOSITE A vintage eiderdown in pretty, soft colours adorns the bed in this old cottage, complementing the beamed ceiling and dark floorboards. Piles of cushions and a fabric-covered canopy with decorative curtains add to the cosy and inviting effect.

TEXTILES

No home is complete without a selection of textiles to inject extra colour, comfort and cosiness. Antique and vintage textiles, in particular, offer a timeless charm and a sense of history that is literally woven into their warp and weft. Look out for holes, tears or stains, but otherwise go to town with these beautiful fabrics, whose faded patina complements both antique furnishings and modern schemes.

OPPOSITE AND RIGHT Panels of antique or vintage lace with delicate, intricate patterns can be turned into stunning window treatments, falling softly and filtering light gently while still providing a sense of warmth and privacy. Drape them over a pole with rippled gathers for a lavish appearance, or create a more minimal look by using a small length as a simple blind/shade.

Curtains and blinds

Using antique or vintage fabrics to make curtains or blinds/shades is a quick way to add colour and individuality to any room. Seek out beautifully textured linen sheets, lengths of lace, Kelsch d'Alsace in red or blue plaid, Swedish ticking or French mattress covers, large linen grain sacks or patchwork Kantha throws; you may even pick up some late 20th-century patterned curtains in a charity shop that can be re-made to the correct size.

A pair of pencil-pleat curtains usually requires plenty of fabric. There are other options, however, if your choice of vintage fabric is not quite large enough to cover a window: a single door curtain, interlined to keep out the draughts, half-height café curtains in sheer linen, small gathered curtains across the fronts of cupboards, or blinds/shades of all kinds for a streamlined or minimal effect.

OPPOSITE Keep out the draughts and add a sumptuous feel to a hallway with a door curtain fashioned from gathered antique linen. Add a deep border to the bottom and a flop-over frill at the top if you wish; a heavy lining will also help keep the house warmer.

ABOVE LEFT Single vintage eiderdowns are much easier to find than doubles, and they make a gorgeous addition to a child's bed or – as in this case – bunk beds. Complementing them is a roll-up blind/shade made from a vintage grain sack, which has a beautiful texture and simple blue stripes.

ABOVE RIGHT As window treatments go, this one is deceptively simple, fitting in perfectly with the white-on-white theme of the room. A pretty lace panel has been draped over a plain cotton tab-top curtain to filter the light and create a barely-there effect.

ABOVE A vintage crochet bedspread makes an effective room divider while prettily complementing the rugged beams and old tiled floor of this ancient cottage.

OPPOSITE These curtains are made from old army blankets – relatively inexpensive and heavy enough that they don't necessarily need lining in order to keep out the draughts. As a contrast, a dark velvet border has been added to the bottoms of the panels, with strips of decorative antique broderie anglaise stitched on top.

Rugs

Art, craft, design and history are all woven together in an antique carpet, rug or runner. Made using hand-spun, naturally dyed yarns in beautiful shades, each one brings a sense of depth and richness to a room, introducing subtle warmth and delicious texture. Look for Persian rugs from the Middle East, Oriental rugs – a definition which includes Turkish rugs and Chinese carpets – and versatile kilims and Swedish flatweave rugs in bold colours and geometric designs.

Where to use them? Anywhere you like. Rugs are an obvious choice for a living room or bedroom, add wonderful softness in a kitchen, bathroom or home office, and are a useful way of establishing different zones within an open-plan space. And don't forget colourful runners to bring life and detail to a narrow hallway.

OPPOSITE The dark background of this vintage floral rug helps delineate the area in front of the wood burner as a cosy spot in which to sit and relax.

LEFT The softly faded colours of a vintage flatweave rug only add to its allure. This example works perfectly in a tranquil bedroom, aligning with the muted shades of antique furniture and pale walls and floor.

BELOW Gently worn, old rugs are easy to source at auction and will generally fit unobtrusively into a room. They provide colour, pattern and softness underfoot, as in this sophisticated, understated bedroom.

LEFT Modest yet beautiful, traditional mattress ticking has a strong, dense, herringbone weave and has been produced for mattress covers throughout Europe and the USA for centuries. It makes excellent curtains, cushions and lots more; use it on its own as a simple accent or to create a balance with plains, florals or other patterns.

OPPOSITE A trio of cushions made from super-soft old French linen provide comfort in the reading nook of this characterful bedroom. They complement the more decorative bedcover, a quilted blue gingham with a block-print backing in contrasting red.

Fabric accents

Aside from window treatments, there are so many ways in which to use vintage textiles around the home. Think of Welsh blankets, faded floral eiderdowns or hand-stitched kantha quilts, warm and welcoming on a bed or over the back of a sofa. Pile up cushions made from Turkish kilims in a variety of colours and patterns or find examples of old knitting or crochet to strike a note of homely, traditional comfort. And check out charity shops and markets for vintage tablecloths with pretty embroidery or lace detailing, perhaps with matching napkins, or a selection of useful tea towels, woven from French linen or printed with 1950s floral motifs.

If you feel up to crafting something yourself, vintage textiles large and small can be repurposed into beautiful and useful items. Cover a headboard or a chair seat, make a lampshade, or stitch cushion covers for a chair, bench or bed. Even tiny scraps could be made into lavender bags or put together as patchwork, while special or fragile pieces can be framed and turned into works of art for your walls.

ABOVE Vintage textiles, whether block-print cotton, embroidered silk or a Japanese kimono, make beautiful displays. Mount them in a large frame or, as here, simply slide them over a slender bamboo pole.

RIGHT In a gentle off-white and with a woven blue stripe, this vintage European grain sack is exactly the right size and shape to use as a textural table runner. Heavy and durable, the sturdy fabric is also machine washable, making it convenient for modern-day life.

ABOVE Beneath a hand-made African feather headdress known as a Juju hat, a quartet of plump vintage kilim cushions offer a delightful variety of soft colours and intricate patterns against a clean white wall.

PAGES 170–171 The quintessentially English architecture of this timber-framed cottage is complemented perfectly by a gorgeous and eclectic mix of French antique and vintage furnishings and textiles, including soft wools, tapestries, linens and cottons. Long curtains would block the light in this low-ceiling room, and the unstructured linen blinds/shades are an ideal solution.

DECORATIVE DETAILS

Our homes are constantly evolving to suit our changing needs and tastes, and smaller, decorative antiques – such as mirrors, ceramics, glassware and works of art – are easily moveable and replaceable, presenting an ideal opportunity to refresh your space without going to great trouble or expense. When you feel like a change, a few carefully chosen such pieces add depth, interest and variety to an interiors scheme.

OPPOSITE An extraordinary, elaborate mirror is just one antique element in this eclectic room, acting as a work of art rather than a means of checking one's reflection.

RIGHT Framed in rattan, sunburst-style mirrors were hugely popular between the 1950s and 1970s. Here, a mass hanging gives them fabulous impact against a plain white wall.

Mirrors

Installing a huge mirror, or several smaller ones, is a great trick if you want to increase the light and sense of space in a room, especially in a hallway or bathroom. Antique and vintage mirrors come in all shapes and sizes, from 18th-century giltwood examples to sunburst rattan styles from the 1970s, via Victorian cheval mirrors, bevel-edge Art Deco, freeform mid-century styles and many more. Some will have a pleasing patina of age caused by the oxidization of the silver backing over time, known as foxing, but, rather than seeing this as a flaw, consider it a pleasing sign of character and individuality.

Large, ornate mirrors can be propped against the wall of a bedroom or hung over the living-room mantelpiece as a luxurious focal point. A small mirror on its own can look lost on a large expanse of wall, so consider arranging several in a group to create more impact. Alternatively, incorporate one or two mirrors into a gallery wall of paintings and prints to add variety to the display.

RIGHT A grouping of mostly inexpensive and modest old mirrors plus a few empty frames creates a sumptuous effect and a dramatic focal point in which the whole is more than the sum of the parts.

BELOW AND OPPOSITE A single very large mirror with an attractive form or pretty, carved detailing will be the focal point in a room and can be stood on the floor or mounted on a wall. As well as having inherent decorative value, it will bounce light around the room beautifully.

ABOVE As mirror glass ages it can show scratches, spots and oxidization, in small areas or extensively. The results can be attractive and don't necessarily detract from its value.

LEFT Although casually hung, this trio of modest artworks possesses a unity of style and framing that creates a lovely cohesion. Their pale backgrounds contrast with the dramatically dark portrait adjacent.

OPPOSITE A large old painting, especially in deep, dramatic colours, can provide an unusual point of interest in a room. The symmetry and scale of the display of antique accessories below this portrait is calm and satisfying.

PAGE 180 Delicately dried, pressed and mounted, framed plants such as these are known as *herbieres*, and often date back to the late 19th or early 20th century. Look out for them in flea markets, antiques shops and online – if necessary, replace worn, cheap or unattractive frames, and group the works together in a linear display.

Art

Vintage art, in all forms and styles from traditional oil paintings to pretty watercolours and monochrome engravings, is readily available wherever antiques are sold. Costs vary from very high end to next to nothing, but it is always best to buy something you love and want to live with, rather than anticipating an increase in value. Consider whether a piece speaks to you in terms of its subject matter, colour and composition, and how it will fit into your home.

A popular technique is to bring together art of different styles, mediums and periods to create an eclectic gallery wall, though you will need to plan out the arrangement with care so that everything is well balanced. Professional picture hangers advise planning your configuration on the floor before reaching for the hammer and nails.

As with mirrors, framing makes an enormous difference to any piece of art. The right frame may be one that matches the style and period of the artwork, but you can also create a dynamic sense of contrast by selecting a traditional frame for a modern painting, or vice versa.

Gathered around a larger contemporary abstract painting are a small collection of vintage artworks, in various styles, that depict boats and harbours, creating a gallery wall that is unified by a subtle and harmonious use of the colour black.

LEFT This vintage stoneware (and some stemmed glass) has been carefully arranged on open shelves so as not to appear too busy or cluttered. The collection includes a pair of Victorian Parian ware 'hand' vases as well as an elegant black basalt coffee pot.

OPPOSITE Shiny ceramic glazes contrast with the distressed paintwork of this antique glazed cabinet. These pieces, plain and patterned, may be useful but they are also intrinsically beautiful.

Ceramics and glassware

Ceramics and glassware are highly collectible, often inexpensive and add instant personality, whether arranged as a display or used on a daily basis.

Lovers of ceramics may well be drawn to blue and white, whether a Willow Pattern tea set or Cornishware striped mugs, but there are many other appealing options, including pretty old-fashioned floral patterns, boldly coloured retro dinner sets and creamy stoneware jugs, bowls and platters. Arrange them on a dresser/hutch, prop them on a sideboard or hang them on the wall: only a few pieces are necessary to create an impact.

Old glassware, too, comes in all shapes and sizes, from 1950s Champagne coupes to mouth-blown wine demijohns. While clear glass fits any decorative scheme, coloured glass provides an infusion of vitality and fun. Whether you prefer the simple functionality of pressed glass or the elegance of hand-cut crystal, such pieces add infinite charm to everyday life.

RIGHT AND BELOW These collections of vintage utilitarian kitchenware, thoughtfully arranged on open shelves, are strictly colour co-ordinated to provide an attractive display as well as being functional pieces for mixing, pouring and serving. Such pieces are easy to track down either on online marketplaces or at antiques fairs and will bring vintage charm to any kitchen.

ABOVE Admirers of antique pressed glass have a plethora of styles from which to choose. An abundance of clear glass objects, as seen here, makes a simple and functional display on an open shelf.

OPPOSITE A dresser heaped with crockery – not necessarily perfectly matching – is always a welcoming sight. The visual interest lies in creating the right mix of colours, patterns, shapes and sizes.

Resources

ANTIQUES FAIRS AND FLEA MARKETS

Antiques Atlas
antiques-atlas.com
This useful website is not only a selling platform, but also has a calendar of antiques fairs plus details of antiques centres in the UK, USA, Australia and Scandinavia.

Antiques News & Fairs
antiquesnews.co.uk
Details of fairs in the UK, Europe and the US.

Brimfield Antique & Flea Markets
Brimfield, MA, USA
brimfieldantiquefleamarket.com
Takes place three times a year in May, July and September.

Rose Bowl Flea Market
Pasadena, CA, USA
rgcshows.com
Takes place on the second Sunday of each month.

Round Top and Warrenton Antique Shows
Round Top and Warrenton, TX, USA
antiqueweekend.com
A twice-yearly antiques festival.

Springfield Antique Show and Flea Market
Springfield, OH, USA
jenkinsandco.com/ springfield-antique-show
Monthly shows plus twice-yearly 'extravaganzas'.

Sunbury Antiques Market
sunburyantiques.com
Held at Kempton Park Racecourse on the second and last Tuesday of every month.

UK Antiques Fairs Calendar
Iacf.co.uk
Antiques fairs around the UK.

BUYING ANTIQUES AND VINTAGE ONLINE

Chairish.com
US curated online marketplace shipping within the continental United States.

Decorativecollective.com
Sellers from the UK and Europe offering a large selection of varied antiques.

Etsy.com
Preowned vintage pieces

Facebook Marketplace
facebook.com/marketplace
Second-hand items for sale.

Freecycle.org
Recycling and exchange website.

Pamono.co.uk
European marketplace for antique and vintage pieces.

Sellingantiques.co.uk
The UK's largest antiques website.

Vinterior.co
More than 2000 sellers of vintage and antique furniture from over 30 countries.

ONLINE AUCTIONS

Auctionet.com
One of Europe's leading auction marketplaces, allowing bidding from anywhere in the world.

Ebay
ebay.co.uk and ebay.com
The original second-hand trading and auction website and a fabulous place to search for antiques and vintage pieces.

The-saleroom.com
A global marketplace offering a wide range of categories to bid on, including antiques and art. Also allows bidding during a live auction.

UK ANTIQUES MARKETS

Alfies Antique Market
13–25 Church Street
London NW8 8DT
alfiesantiques.com

Dairy House Antiques Dorset
Station Road, Semley
Shaftesbury
Dorset SP7 9AN
dairyhouseantiques.com

Hemswell Antiques Centre
Caenby Corner Estate
Hemswell Cliff
Gainsborough
Lincolnshire DN21 5TJ
hemswell-antiques.com

Hungerford Antiques Arcade
26–27 High Street
Hungerford
Berkshire RG17 0NF
hungerfordarcade.com

Lorfords Antiques
30 Long Street
Tetbury
Gloucestershire GL8 8AQ
lorfordsantiques.com

The Old Cinema
160 Chiswick High Road
London W4 1PR
theoldcinema.co.uk

The Old Flight House
Northampton Road,
Bicester
Oxfordshire OX25 3TJ
theoldflighthouse.co.uk

Petworth Antiques Market
East Street
Petworth
West Sussex GU28 0AB
petworthantiquesmarket.com

Portobello Road Market
Portobello Road
London W10 5RU
visitportobello.com
Saturday is the best day for antiques hunters.

Preston Antique Centre
The Mill, New Hall Lane
Preston
Lancashire PR1 5NQ
prestonantiquecentre.co.uk

St Martins Antiques Centre
23a High Street
Stamford
Lincolnshire PE9 2LF
st-martins-antiques.co.uk

Station Mill Antiques Centre
Station Road
Chipping Norton
Oxfordshire OX7 5HX
stationmill.com

US ANTIQUES STORES AND MARKETS

fleamapket.com
A handy app that offers a directory of antique stores and flea markets.

Flea Market Zone
Fleamarketzone.com
The largest flea market and swap meet directory in the US.

Kovels Antique Trader
Antiquetrader.com
A directory of antique stores and malls throughout the US and Canada.

Picture credits

Endpapers ph. Jan Baldwin/The home of Melanie Molesworth, freelance interiors stylist 1 ph. Ben Edwards/The home of Jon and Louise Bunning of Mora Lifestyle, Norwich; 2–3 ph. Rachel Whiting/The Dorset home of Libby Rose of @atelierelizabethrose; 4 ph. Polly Wreford/Alba Beach House, Cornwall. Available to rent through Unique Homestays uniquehomestays.com; 5 ph. Polly Wreford/Openview Barn at Foster House, designed by Atlanta Bartlett and Dave Coote, available to hire for photography through beachstudios.co.uk; 7 ph. Debi Treloar/The family home of Harriet Maxwell Macdonald of Ochre.net in New York; 8–9 ph. Benjamin Edwards/The home of Louise Miller in London, available to hire through www.millerstyle.co.uk; 10 ph. Polly Wreford/A family home in Islington designed by Nicola Harding; 13 ph. Ben Edwards/The London home of Emma Gurmin; 14–15 ph. Anna Williams/The home of the designer Yvonne Koné in Copenhagen; 16 ph. Benjamin Edwards/The home of Louise Miller in London, available to hire through www.millerstyle.co.uk; 17 ph. Tom Leighton; 18 above ph. Anna Williams/The home of the designer Josephine Ekström, owner of Lily & Oscar, in Sweden; 18 below ph. Polly Wreford/The Sawmills Studios; 19 ph. Benjamin Edwards/The home of Lori Guyer, owner of White Flower Farmhouse, in Greenport, New York; 20 ph. Jan Baldwin/The home of fashion designer Mr Antoni Burakowski & hair stylist Mr Kerry Warn in London; 21 ph. Rachel Whiting/The home of Bella and Hugo Middleton, norfolknaturalliving.com; 22 left ph. Pia Ulin/The home of Marzio Cavanna in Milan; 22 right ph. Debi Treloar/Fred Musik; 23 ph. Polly Wreford/Interior design by Nicola Harding & Co.; 24 ph. Debi Treloar/Fred Musik; 25 above ph. Tom Leighton/Keith Varty & Alan Cleaver's apartment in London, designed by Jonathan Reed; 25 below left ph. Rachel Whiting/The home of Bella and Hugo Middleton, norfolknaturalliving.com; 25 below right ph. Ben Edwards/The home of the designer and embroiderer Caroline Zoob in Sussex; 26 ph Polly Wreford/an apartment in New York, designed by Belmont Freeman Architects; 27 ph. Polly Wreford/The home of Ben Baglio and Richard Wilson in Suffolk www.benbaglio.com; 28 ph. James Gardiner/Jeska and Dean Hearne www.thefuturekept.com; 29 ph. Debi Treloar/The home of interior stylist Deborah Vos www.deborahvos.com; 30 ph. Catherine Gratwicke/Barbara Bestor, www.bestorarchitecture.com; 31 ph. Catherine Gratwicke/The home of Pien Essink of Studio Pien, The Netherlands; 32 ph. Rachel Whiting/Jonathan Lo www.happymundane.com; 33 above left ph Tom Leighton/interior designer Philip Hooper's own house in East Sussex; 33 above right ph. Jan Baldwin/interior designer Philip Hooper's own house in East Sussex; 33 below ph. Andrew Wood/Norma Holland's house in London; 34 ph. Dan Duchars/Anneke Herbers and Marjon Herbers, herberslifestyle.nl; 35 ph. Debi Treloar/The home of Mark and Sally Bailey of baileyshome.com; 36 above right ph. Dan Duchars/Harriet's shed in Herefordshire, @yomargey; 36 below left ph. Dan Duchars/Llednant Farmhouse, available to rent through Unique Homestays; 36 below right ph. Debi Treloar/The home of designer Anna Phillips & Jeff Kightly – owners of knitwear company Hambro & Miller www.hambroandmiller.co.uk; 37 ph. Debi Treloar/The home of Antonio Bembo and Anda Hobai in Romania; 38 above ph. Polly Wreford/The home of Ben Baglio and Richard Wilson in Suffolk www.benbaglio.com; 38 below ph. Ben Edwards/The home of Jon and Louise Bunning of Mora Lifestyle, Norwich; 39 ph. Debi Treloar/Kvarngården. The home of photographer Nils Odier, stylist Sofia Odier and their two daughters Lou and Uma. Skivarp, Sweden; 40 ph. Polly Wreford/Interior design by Nicola Harding & Co.; 41 ph. Rachel Whiting/The home of interior journalist and blogger Jill Macnair in London; 42 ph. Debi Treloar/Tina B; 45 ph. Anna Williams/The Brooklyn loft of Alina Preciado owner of lifestyle store dar gitane www.dargitane.com; 46 ph. Catherine Gratwicke/The home of production designer Misty Buckley www.mistybuckley.com; 47 above ph. Polly Wreford/The Sawmills Studios; 47 below ph. Pia Ulin/The home of Giorgio DeLuca in New York; 48 above left ph. Benjamin Edwards/The home of Louise Miller in London, available to hire through www.millerstyle.co.uk; 48 above right ph Catherine Gratywicke; 48 below left ph. Polly Wreford/L'Atelier d'Archi - Isabelle Juy – www.latelierarchi.fr; 48 below right ph. Benjamin Edwards/The home of Louise Miller in London, available to hire through www.millerstyle.co.uk; 49 ph. Polly Wreford/Alba Beach House, Cornwall. Available to rent through Unique Homestays uniquehomestays.com; 50 ph. Catherine Gratwicke/The home of

Manonne & Remco in Heemstede, The Netherlands; 51 ph. Debi Treloar/Clapton Tram, the home of John Bassam, in Hackney available to hirewww.claptontram.com; 52–53 ph. Rachel Whiting/The home of Genevieve Harris in Kent; 54–55 ph. Ben Edwards/The home of Jon and Louise Bunning of Mora Lifestyle, Norwich; 56 above ph. Catherine Gratwicke/The family home of Gina Portman of Folk at Home www.folkathome.com; 56 below left ph. Ben Edwards/The home and homestead of Stephanie Eley in Oxfordshire; 56 below right ph.Polly Wreford/ Glenn Carwithen & Sue Miller's house in London; 57 ph. Ben Edwards/Susannah and Mark Adorian; 58 ph. Jan Baldwin/Bridget Elworthy www.thelandgardeners.com; 59 above ph. Debi Treloar/The home of Mark and Sally Bailey of baileyshome.com; 59 below ph. Jan Baldwin/The London home of Lulu Lytle of Soane Britain www.soane.com; 60 ph. Catherine Gratwicke/Agnes Emery's house in Brussels; tiles and drawer handles from Emery & Cie; 61 ph. Polly Wreford/The home of family Voors in the Netherlands designed by Karin Draaijer; 62 ph. Jan Baldwin/The home of fashion designer Mr Antoni Burakowski & hair stylist Mr Kerry Warn in London; 63 ph. Benjamin Edwards/Home of Justine Hand, contributing editor Remodelista, on Cape Cod; 64 left ph. Rachel Whiting/The family home of Justina Blakeney in Los Angeles; 64 above right ph. Catherine Gratwicke/Agnes Emery's house in Brussels; tiles, star light and drawer handles from Emery & Cie; 64 below right ph. Benjamin Edwards/Home of Justine Hand, contributing editor Remodelista, on Cape Cod; 65 ph. Jan Baldwin/The home of Gavin Waddell; 66 ph. Jan Baldwin/The Home of Lucy Bathurst of Nest Design www.nestdesign.co.uk; 68 ph. Debi Treloar/London home of Eloise Jones & Aine Donovan; 69 ph. Jan Baldwin/The home of fashion designer Mr Antoni Burakowski & hair stylist Mr Kerry Warn in London; 70 above ph. Pia Ulin/The home of Adriana Natcheva, Groves Natcheva Architects; 70 below ph. Andrew Wood/media executive's house in LA, architect: Stephen Slan, builder: Ken Duran, furnishings: Russell Simpson, original architect: Carl Maston c.1945.; 71 ph. Catherine Gratwicke/The home of Matthew and Gillian Chessé; 72 ph. Debi Treloar/The home of Einar Jone Rønning and Siv Eline, owner of the gallery www.TM51.no in Oslo; 73 above ph. Andrew Wood/Norma Holland's house in London; 73 below ph. Paul Ryan/Architect: Peter Hulting www.meterarkitektur.se; 74 above ph. Dan Duchars/Llednant Farmhouse, available to rent through Unique Homestays; 74 below ph. Andrew Wood/Heidi Kingstone's apartment in London; 75 ph. Polly Wreford/Alba Beach House, Cornwall. Available to rent through Unique Homestays uniquehomestays.com; 76 ph. Debi Treloar/Interior designers Stefan & Jeanette Walther of home-interior.de; 77 above left ph. Dan Duchars/Llednant Farmhouse, available to rent through Unique Homestays; 77 above right ph. Polly Wreford/The Sawmills Studios; 77 below left ph. Polly Wreford/A family home in West London by Webb Architects and Cave Interiors; 77 below right ph. Rachel Whiting/Karine Köng, founder and Creative Director of online concept store BODIE and FOU www.bodieandfou.com; 78 ph. Polly Wreford/The home of Victoria and Stephen Fordham, designed by Sarah Delaney, in London; 80 ph. Benjamin Edwards/Home of Justine Hand, contributing editor Remodelista, on Cape Cod; 81 ph. Benjamin Edwards/The home of Lisa Brass of Design Vintage; 82 ph. Jan Baldwin/The home of fashion designer Mr Antoni Burakowski & hair stylist Mr Kerry Warn in London; 83 above ph. Andrew Wood/media executive's house in LA, architect: Stephen Slan, builder: Ken Duran, furnishings: Russell Simpson, original architect: Carl Maston c.1945.; 83 below ph. Polly Wreford/Josephine Ryan Antiques in Tetbury, josephineryanantiques.myshopify.com; 84 ph. Catherine Gratwicke/Tracy Wilkinson www.twworkshop.com; 85 ph. Jan Baldwin/Jo Scofield and Andrew Yarme in Bristol; 86 ph. Ben Edwards/Michelle Essam's home In Sussex; 87 ph. Lisa Cohen; 88 above ph. Tom Leighton; 88 below left ph. Ben Edwards/Rosehip in the Country www.rosehipinthecountry.com; 88 below right ph. Polly Wreford/The Sussex home of Paula Barnes of www.elzabarnes.com; 89 ph. Anna Williams/The home Leida Nassir-Pour of Warp & Weft in Hastings/ph. Claire Richardson; 90–91 ph. Debi Treloar/The home of Whinnie Williams of www.poodleandblonde.com; 93 ph. Jan Baldwin/The home of Anita Evagora and David Campbell; 94–95 ph. Anna Williams/Bea B&B owned by Bea Mombaers in Knokke-Le Zoute, Belgium www.bea-bb.com; 96 left ph. Jan Baldwin/The Home of Lucy Bathurst of Nest Design www.nestdesign.co.uk; 96 right ph. Jan Baldwin/The Dorset home of Edward & Jane Hurst; 97 ph. Jan Baldwin/The home of Frank Hollmeyer and Robert Weems; 98 above ph. Debi Treloar/The home of interior stylist Deborah Vos www.deborahvos.com; **98 below** ph. Andrew Wood/Kurt Bredenbeck's apartment in the Barbican, London; **99** ph. Jan Baldwin/A Georgian terraced house in London, designed by Robert and Josyane Young for Riviere Interiors www.robertyoungantiques.com; **100** ph. Jan Baldwin/Melanie Molesworth freelance interiors stylist; **101 above left** ph. Anna Williams/The Brooklyn loft of Alina Preciado owner of lifestyle store dar gitane www.dargitane.com; **101 above right** ph. Polly Wreford/The London home of designer Suzy Radcliffe; **101 below** ph. Polly Wreford/The Cheshire home of architect and interior designer Annabelle Tugby, www.annabelletugbyarchitects.co.uk; **101 below right** ph. Andrew Wood/John Chiem's apartment in New York; **102** ph. Benjamin Edwards/The home of Lisa Brass of Design Vintage; **104** ph. Rachel Whiting/The home of interior designer Anna Haines www.annahaines.com; **105** ph. Rachel Whiting/Paul West, @consideredthings; **106 left** ph. Anna Williams/The home Leida Nassir-Pour of Warp & Weft in Hastings/ph. Claire Richardson; **106 right** ph. Polly Wreford/The Cheshire home of architect and interior designer Annabelle Tugby, www.annabelletugbyarchitects.co.uk; **107** ph. Polly Wreford/ Ros Fairman's house in London; **108 above left** ph. Andrew Wood/Alastair Hendy & John Clinch's apartment in London, designed by Alastair Hendy; **108 above right** ph. Benjamin Edwards/The Old Coastguard House – home of Martin and Jane Will; **108 below** ph. Catherine Gratwicke/Ellis Flytes house in London; **109** ph. Benjamin Edwards/Architects and homeowners Mette Fredskild and Masahiro Katsume; **110–111** ph. Debi Treloar/Pip Rau www.piprau. com piprau@mac.com; **112** ph. Polly Wreford/The family home of Sacha Paisley in Sussex, designed by Arior Design; **113** ph. Debi Treloar/The home of Jo Wood, founder of jowoodorganics.com; **114 above left & below** ph. Catherine Gratwicke/the brownstone in New York of Bonnie Young, director of global sourcing and inspiration at Donna Karan International; **115** ph. Dan Duchars/ Batman's Summerhouse in Devon, available to rent at twocabins.com; **116** ph. Benjamin Edwards/Designer James van der Velden of Bricks Studio, Amsterdam; **117 above left** ph. Benjamin Edwards/The home of @susliving in Denmark; **117 below left** ph. Anna Williams/The home Leida Nassir-Pour of Warp & Weft in Hastings/ph. Claire Richardson; **117 right** ph. Jan Baldwin/Jo Scofield and Andrew Yarme in Bristol; **118** ph. Polly Wreford/The home of Victoria and Stephen Fordham, designed by Sarah Delaney, in London; **119** ph. Benjamin Edwards/ The home of Kay Prestney @kinship_creativedc; **120** ph. Catherine Gratwicke/ The home of production designer Misty Buckley www.mistybuckley.com; **121** ph. Rachel Whiting/Sophie Rowell, interior consultant @ Côte de Folk, www.cotedefolk.com; **122 above left** ph. Chris Everard/Sera Hersham-Loftus' house in London; **122 above right** ph. Benjamin Edwards/The home of Kay Prestney @kinship_creativedc; **122 below** ph. Polly Wreford/A family home in West London by Webb Architects and Cave Interiors www.caveinteriors.com; **123** ph. Jan Baldwin/Egford House is the home of Liddie & Howard Holt Harrison; **124–125** ph. Rachel Whiting/The home of interior journalist and blogger Jill Macnair in London; **127** ph. Ben Edwards/A country cottage in Suffolk, the home of Amanda and Belle Daughtry; **128** ph. Rachel Whiting/Paul West, @consideredthings; **129** ph. Polly Wreford/The home of interior designer Caroline Van Thillo in Belgium; **130** ph. Debi Treloar/Bryncyn is available for holiday rental at http://thewelshhouse.org; **131 above left** ph. Tom Leighton; **131 above right** ph. Tom Leighton/a loft in London, designed by Robert Dye Associates; **131 below left** ph. Andrew Wood/Brian Johnson's apartment in London, designed by Johnson Naylor; **131 below right** ph. Catherine Gratwicke/ a New York City apartment, designed by Marino + Giolito; **132 left** ph. Anna Williams/The B&B Camellas-Lloret, designed and owned by Annie Moore near Carcassonne/ph.Claire Richardson; **132 right** ph. Anna Williams/The home of Jocie Sinauer owner of Red Chair on Warren in Hudson, New York; **133** ph. Hans Blomquist; **134** ph. Debi Treloar/The home of Shelley Carline, owner of the shop Hilary and Flo in Sheffield; **135** ph. Polly Wreford/The home in Copenhagen of designer Birgitte Raben Olrik of Raben Saloner; **136** ph. Andrew Woods/a house in London, designed by Guy Stansfield; **137** ph. Andrew Wood; **138 left** ph. Jan Baldwin/The Norwich Studio and home of Carol Lake www.carollake.co.uk; **138 above right** ph. Ben Edwards/The home of the designer and embroiderer Caroline Zoob in Sussex; **138 below right** ph. Rachel Whiting/Victoria Smith editor sfgirlbybay.com; **139** ph. Jan Baldwin/Kim Wilkie's London flat; **140** ph. Rachel Whiting/The seaside home of designer Marta Nowicka, available to rent www.martanowicka.com; **141** ph. Dan Duchars/Llednant Farmhouse, available to

rent through Unique Homestays; **142 above left** ph. Debi Treloar/The home of Helene & Robin of Neilson Boutique in Cuckfield, Sussex www.neilsonboutique. co.uk; **142 below** ph. Tom Leighton; **143** ph. Polly Wreford/Coastal House Devon, 6a. Architects; **145** ph. Debi Treloar/ The London home of James Waters Producer and Yolanda Chiaramallo floral designer and photographer; **146** ph. Catherine Gratwicke/Oliver Heath and Katie Weiner – sustainable architecture, interior and jewellery design; **147** ph. Polly Wreford/The home of interior designer Caroline Van Thillo in Belgium; **148 above left** ph. Rachel Whiting/ Victoria Smith editor sfgirlbybay.com; **148 above right** ph. Rachel Whiting/The home of artist/interiors consultant Russell Loughlan; **148 below left** ph. Fritz von der Schulenburg; **148 below right** ph. Polly Wreford; **149** ph. Catherine Gratwicke/The home of Manonne & Remco in Heemstede, The Netherlands; **150** ph. Hans Blomquist/The Swedish home of interior stylist and decorator Marie Olsson Nylander; **151** ph. Benjamin Edwards/Designer James van der Velden of Bricks Studio, Amsterdam; **152** ph. Catherine Gratwicke/The Madrid home of the interior designer Patricia Bustos de la Torre Instagram.com/ patricia_bustos, www.patricia-bustos.com; **153 above left** ph. Polly Wreford/ home of 27:12 Design Ltd, Chelsea, NYC; **153 below left** ph. Polly Wreford/The family home of Elisabeth and Scott Wotherspoon, owners of Wickle in Lewes, www.wickle.co.uk; **153 right** ph. Polly Wreford/home of 27:12 Design Ltd, Chelsea, NYC; **155** ph. Simon Brown; **156** ph. Debi Treloar/The home of Jo Wood, founder of jowoodorganics.com; **157** ph. Debi Treloar/The home of Jo Wood, founder of jowoodorganics.com; **158** ph. Benjamin Edwards/The home and homestead of Stephanie Eley in Oxfordshire; **159 left** ph. Benjamin Edwards/ The London home of Emma Gurmin; **159 right** ph. Polly Wreford/Paul and Claire's beach house in East Sussex. Design www.davecoote.com, location available to hire through www.beachstudios.co.uk; **160** ph. Benjamin Edwards/ Rosehip in the Country www.rosehipinthecountry.com; **161** ph. Jan Baldwin/The home of Lucy Bathurst of Nest Design; **162** ph. Rachel Whiting/The home of designers Jessie Cutts and Ivo Vos in Kent, cuttandsons.com; **163** ph. Rachel Whiting/The home of Bella and Hugo Middleton, norfolknaturalliving.com; **164** ph. Debi Treloar/Retrouvius.com; **165 above** ph. Rachel Whiting/The home of artist/interiors consultant Russell Loughlan; **166** ph. Debi Treloar/The home of Mark & Sally Bailey www.baileyshome.com; **167** ph. Benjamin Edwards/ Rosehip in the Country www.rosehipinthecountry.com; **168 above** ph. Benjamin Edwards/Interior stylist and graphic designer Pernille Grønkjaer Taato of Nordidskrum.dk in Denmark; **168 below** ph. Jan Baldwin/Elizabeth Machin's Norfolk cottage; **169** ph. Katya de Grunwald/Sara Schmidt, owner and creative director of Brandts Indoor; **170–171** ph. Benjamin Edwards/ Rosehip in the Country www.rosehipinthecountry.com; **173** ph. Polly Wreford/The home of interior designer Sarah Lavoine in Paris; **174** ph. Anna Williams/The home Leida Nassir-Pour of Warp & Weft in Hastings/ph. Claire Richardson; **175** ph. Rachel Whiting/Designed by Stephane Garotin and Pierre Emmanuel Martin of Maison Hand in Lyon; **176 above** ph. Anna Williams/The home of Jocie Sinauer owner of Red Chair on Warren in Hudson, New York; **176 below left** ph. Polly Wreford/ Clare Nash's house in London; **176 below right** ph. Debi Treloar/The home of designer Anna Phillips & Jeff Kightly – owners of knitwear company Hambro & Miller www.hambroandmiller.co.uk; **177** ph. Ben Edwards/The home in Arundel of John Taylor and Barbara Cunnell of Woodpigeon; **178** ph. Polly Wreford/The home in Lewes of Justin & Heidi Francis, owner of Flint, www.flintcollection. com; **179** ph. Rachel Whiting/The home of Genevieve Harris in Kent; **180** ph. Ben Edwards/The London home of Emma Gurmin; **181** ph. Rachel Whiting/The home of artist/interiors consultant Russell Loughlan; **182** ph. Benjamin Edwards/ Home of Justine Hand, contributing editor at Remodelista, on Cape Cod; **183** ph. Benjamin Edwards/ Rosehip in the Country www.rosehipinthecountry.com; **184 above** ph. Ben Edwards/The home in Arundel of John Taylor and Barbara Cunnell of Woodpigeon; **184 below left** ph. Anna Williams/The home of Jocie Sinauer, owner of Red Chair on Warren in Hudson, New York; **184 below right** ph. Anna Williams/ANON; **185** ph. Jan Baldwin/The home of Jack Brister and Richard Nares in Frome, Somerset; **186** ph. Anna Williams/The Brooklyn loft of Alina Preciado, owner of lifestyle store dar gitane www.dargitane.com; **189** ph. Polly Wreford/Ann Shore's house in London.

Index